Presented

From:

Date:

Make Your Day Count Devotional

for Women

Presented by
Lindsay Roberts and Friends

Harrison House
Tulsa, Oklahoma

Make Your Day Count Devotional for Women
ISBN 1-57794-365-1
Copyright © 2004 by Lindsay Roberts
Oral Roberts Ministries
Tulsa, OK 74171-0001

Published by **Harrison House, Inc.**
P.O. Box 35035
Tulsa, OK 74153

Manuscript compiled and edited by Betsy Williams of Williams Services, Inc., Tulsa, Oklahoma; www.williams.services.inc@cox.net.

Contents

Introduction

Chances are, you're like me—you lead a busy life with many demanding responsibilities. Your days are filled from sunup to sundown and your to-do list is never-ending. But do your days always get off to a good start?

What we do first thing in the morning sets the tone for the rest of the day. The purpose of this book is to give you a bite-sized bit of godly wisdom shared by some of the most outstanding women in the Body of Christ today. Then we've included an action step, something practical you can do each day to apply what you've learned.

Sprinkled throughout you will find some helpful hints and mouth-watering recipes you are sure to enjoy. My goal, and that of the other contributors, is to help you start each day on the right track and *make your day count!*

Blessings,
Lindsay

The Power of God's Love

Lindsay Roberts

Everyone who loves has been born of God and knows God.
Whoever does not love does not know God, because
God is love.

—1 John 4:7,8

God is love, and everyone who knows Him knows love. That means the words *God* and *love* are synonymous. Once I heard Kenneth Copeland say that every time you see the word *God* in Scripture, you can replace it with the word *love* and vice versa.

Take 1 John 4:18, for example, which says, "Perfect love drives out fear." You could exchange the word *love* for *God*, and then it would say, "God drives out fear."

If God is the highest power of all powers and it takes His love to get rid of fear, think about how powerful fear can be. Then it's easy to see how it keeps people in bondage. But the love of God is more powerful than anything. It can calm any situation and bring peace and hope instead.

Some people think that love is all about hearts and flowers. But getting through the tough situations in life takes more than a box of candy and a greeting card!

God's love is powerful! When you understand the power of love and ask God to pour it out through you to those around you, you can become a bridge over troubled waters. Regardless of what you face today, I encourage you to pull out your secret weapon of love.[1]

make **your** day count

Make your day count! Declare, "Nothing I face today is bigger than God and His love for me. As I give place to His love, I will overcome every obstacle and be a vessel of His love to others."

Come on Out Into the Deep!

Joyce Meyer

[Jesus] said unto Simon, Launch out into the deep,
and let down your nets for a draught.

—Luke 5:4 KJV

The beginning and the end of projects are exciting, but the middle usually isn't. Yet that's where we find out if we're truly men and women of God.

Jesus told Simon to launch out into the deep, but Simon Peter replied, "Master, we have toiled all the night, and have taken nothing" (v. 5). The fishermen were exhausted and disappointed, yet Jesus wanted them to go out again, deeper.

Do you know what "the deep" is? It is no longer living by what *you want*, what *you think*, or what *you feel*. It means laying all that aside and doing what *God* said to do, when *He* said to do it, the way *He* said to do it—whether you feel like it or not.

The devil might be screaming, "Why are you doing this? You're stupid, and it's not working!" That's when you have to dig way down deep inside and find out what God said to you, then do it because He told you to.

You may have lost hope in your heart for completing half-finished projects, but God is saying, *It's not too late. You gave up, but I never gave up.* When you follow God's directions and launch out into the deep, blessings will start coming your way. Be like the apostle Paul and finish your course with joy! (Acts 20:24.)[2]

make **your** day count

Make your day count! Take any half-finished situations
off the shelf of your heart, and submit them to God today.
He will help you finish them so that you can receive the prize.

Extreme Lengths

Terri Copeland Pearsons

[Jesus said], "I lay down my life for the sheep."
—John 10:15

Jesus went to extreme lengths to prove God's love to even the most sinful men. Luke 8 tells of a time when He had ministered all day, then got into a boat to go over to the other side. It wasn't an easy trip. They encountered hurricane force winds until Jesus rebuked the storm, putting a stop to it.

When they arrived, a man met them who was so full with evil spirits that he could not be bound—a man who lived in the tombs, thriving off bodies and carcasses, cutting and beating himself. He ran toward Jesus, probably intending to kill Him, but when he ran into the presence of God, those demonic powers fell in subjection. Jesus drove out the demons and set him free.

Think about the extremes Jesus went to. Why did He travel across the lake when He was so tired that He fell asleep shortly after setting sail? Why did He go through the storm? I'm convinced it's because God heard the cry of one desperate man and said to Jesus, "I don't care how bound up by perversion he is or what he looks, smells, or acts like. I love him. Go and set him free."

God hears your cry too, and He has gone to great extremes to purchase your freedom. Be set free today![3]

make **your** day count

Make your day count! Meditate on the extremes that Jesus went to in order to set you free, and take hold of that freedom today!

Your Ultimate Line of Defense

Dee Simmons

I will not die but live, and will proclaim
what the LORD has done.

—Psalm 118:17

"You have cancer." Those three words are life changing to everyone who hears them. The lump in my breast was discovered during a routine exam in 1987, and although the resulting surgery was successful, the episode was a wake-up call for me.

I had been a churchgoer, prayed daily, and gave generously, but I had wandered from the strong spiritual moorings my parents provided for me. They instilled in me the Word of God and the importance of a personal relationship with Him. I had been blessed with a life of luxury, but now I faced a terrifying truth—without God at the center of my life, I had nothing.

Medically, I recovered quickly, but God's plan for me involved far more. As well as reconnecting with God through a more intimate relationship with Him, I became an avid student of nutrition. I believed that if you took the best from science and the best from nature, the result would be the foundation for a healthy life. *This will become a ministry to people around the world*, God told me, and it has.

Taking charge of our physical health is certainly important, but our ultimate line of defense is to join our spirits with that of the living God. He wants us to be healthy, whole, and strong in every area of our lives.[4]

make **your** day count

Make your day count! Whether you are in need of
healing or you are experiencing excellent health,
determine to put your relationship with God first today,
thanking Him for being your ultimate line of defense.

time **saving** tips

Tips To Make Your Day Count

Dee Simmons

 Strawberries usually emit a fruit gas, so when picking ripe strawberries, you should be able to smell their sweet flavor.

 To ripen most fruit, store it in a brown paper bag to trap the fruit gases. This can cause the fruit to ripen up to ten times faster.

Dee's Strawberry Salad[5]

Dee Simmons

Salad:
2 bags salad mix
$\frac{1}{2}$ bag baby spinach
2 pints strawberries, sliced
2 cups Monterey Jack cheese, grated
$\frac{1}{2}$ cup sliced almonds

Dressing:
1 cup olive oil
$\frac{1}{2}$ cup red vinegar
$\frac{1}{8}$ cup sugar
$\frac{1}{2}$ tsp. salt
2 cloves garlic, crushed
$\frac{1}{4}$ tsp. pepper
$\frac{1}{2}$ tsp. paprika

Brown sliced almonds in 350° oven for 2–3 minutes.
Mix salad greens and add almonds, strawberries, and cheese.
Mix dressing; add to salad. Toss and serve.

Loving the Woman in the Mirror

Taffi L. Dollar

[We] continued to behold [in the Word of God]
as in a mirror the glory of the Lord, are constantly
being transfigured into His very own image.

—2 Corinthians 3:18 AMP

God has a specific assignment for you. Your ability to
fulfill this plan, however, depends on how you see yourself.
Your self-image must line up with God's image in order for
you to successfully accomplish His purpose for your life.

You must make a decision. Do you want to look and live
like the world or conform to God's ideal image of you? Is
your self-perception based on someone else's opinion of you
or God's opinion? We should be more concerned about what
God thinks and learn to appreciate the women He has made
us to be.

We can learn a lot from Adam and Eve. Although they
were perfectly created in God's image, they weren't satisfied.
They wanted to improve what God had already made perfect.
Genesis 1:26 tells us that God made us in His image, after
His likeness, but Adam and Eve lost sight of this truth.

The devil conned them into thinking that God had short-
changed them. He said, "God knows that when you eat of it

your eyes will be opened, and you will be like God" (Gen. 3:5). The truth is, Adam and Eve were *already* like God!

Are you attempting to become what you already are? You should never be ashamed of the woman you see in the mirror. You are beautiful in God's eyes, created in His image! Begin to see yourself that way.[6]

make **your** day count

Make your day count! Look in the mirror today,
and affirm that you are made in God's image,
after His likeness. God loves the woman He sees. Do you?

Godly Discipline for the Family

Evelyn Roberts

Discipline your son, and he will give you peace;
he will bring delight to your soul.

—Proverbs 29:17

There is no greater proof of your love for your children than correctly applied discipline. Discipline involves more than punishment. It also includes guiding, teaching, and directing their lives. I believe that if you discipline your children with a mixture of firmness and love, set guidelines for their protection, and give them direction and teaching from God's Word, they will "rise up and call [you] blessed," (Prov. 31:28 AMP).

I especially encourage parents to set aside a specific time for their family to read the Bible, pray, or just enjoy being together. When you gather as a family to center your hearts and minds on God, you are bringing your children into the presence of God Himself. You will also gain a new strength, a new wisdom, and a deeper love for one another. Family devotions, Bible memory verses, or taking turns giving the blessing before meals are ways to share God's presence.

The responsibility of rearing children is awesome and not to be taken lightly. Again and again, while my children were growing up, I turned to God to supply sensitivity, wisdom, and insight for me as their parent. It is not a sign of weakness to call upon God for help. Rather, it is wise to seek His guidance.[7]

make **your** day count

Make your day count! Discipline is guiding, teaching, and directing your children's lives. In what way can you do this today?

time **saving** tips

Tips To Make Your Day Count

You can line the inside doors of your kitchen cabinets with self-stick cork tiles and turn them into bulletin boards. They are great for holding take-out menus, favorite recipes, emergency telephone numbers, and more![8]

A great way to enjoy the photos you receive from family and loved ones at Christmas is to mount a bulletin board in a place where you will see it often and neatly organize the photos on it. Each Christmas, remove the photos from the previous year and begin putting up new ones.

On a bulletin board, you can use straight pins instead of thumbtacks and pushpins to hang photos. The pins don't detract from the photos, yet they do the same trick.

easy **recipes**

Simple Rice Pilaf[9]

Evelyn Roberts

1 pkg. dry chicken noodle soup mix
2 cups water
1 cup dry rice (uncooked), preferably brown rice
2 Tbsp. margarine

- In a pot put 2 cups water and the flavor packet from the package of dry soup. Bring to a boil.
- In a skillet put the margarine and the noodles from the package. Sauté until golden brown.
- Remove from heat and pour in dry rice. Stir and let it soak up remainder of margarine.
- Put both soup mixture and rice/noodle mixture in casserole with lid.
- Place in 350° oven for 1 hour. Do not stir.
- If you use brown rice, it may take an extra 15 minutes to become tender.

- Note: This is a recipe my family has enjoyed for many years. Very simple. Can be used with many things: chicken, steak, pork chops, beef, etc.

Be Filled and Spilled!

Marilyn Hickey

After they prayed, the place where they were meeting
was shaken. And they were all filled with the
Holy Spirit and spoke the word of God boldly.

—Acts 4:31

God wants to fill you with His Spirit for a purpose. We see this in the book of Acts when many wonderful miracles were performed through believers after they were filled with the Spirit.

If you put a dry sponge in water, it soaks up the water. Likewise, we "soak up" the Spirit. But when the sponge is filled, it drips. Many who are filled with the Spirit never let the anointing spill out of them; they just drip. On the other hand, you can squeeze the sponge, releasing and spilling the water. God doesn't want drips; He wants spills!

The apostle Peter gives us a good example in Acts 2. He had denied Christ, yet on the Day of Pentecost, full of the Holy Spirit, he preached to the multitude. Three thousand were saved!

Peter was initially filled with the Spirit in Acts 2:4. But Acts 4:8 KJV says, "Peter, filled with the Holy Ghost...." Again in verse 31 it says about Peter and others, "They were all filled with the Holy Ghost." Notice that these fillings happened *after* the initial outpouring. *There are more fillings!* When you get spilled, you have to get filled again.

God wants to use you to minister to others, so don't be a drip. Get filled with the Holy Spirit, and then spill Him onto everyone you meet.[10]

make **your** day count

Make your day count! Fill up on the Holy Spirit today and allow Him to spill out onto those who need a touch from God.

Just Say Yes!

Lindsay Roberts

No matter how many promises God has made,
they are "Yes" in Christ.

—2 Corinthians 1:20

When I was eighteen, I was told that I would never have children. Today I have three daughters—all miracles—but they did not come easily. Before I received my miracles, I had miscarriages, a tumor, and the death of a baby son.

I finally had to come to a place that instead of saying, "God heals people," I had to say, "God heals *me*." It was when I made a decision to believe in healing for myself that the miracles began.

In John 5:1–15, Jesus approached a man who had been waiting thirty-eight years by the Pool of Bethesda for an angel to stir the water so he could be healed. In thirty-eight years, the man had not figured out how to be the first into the pool to be healed! He was just waiting and wondering.

Jesus asked him, "Do you want to get well?" (v. 6). Instead of saying yes, the man replied, "I have no one to [put] me into the pool" (v. 7). Jesus looked for people who would answer, "Yes! I believe!"

Today we have the same opportunity. Instead of saying, "I don't have anyone to help me," or, "God heals people but He hasn't healed me," we must say, "Yes! I believe I receive my healing." Then we must stay expectant in faith until the miracle comes.[11]

make **your** day count

Make your day count! Whatever miracle you need today,
know that God wants to perform it. Say, "Yes! I believe
Your promise concerning my need. Yes, You are talking to me!"

Transformed from the Inside Out

Kate McVeigh

Let God transform you into a new person by changing
the way you think. Then you will know what God
wants you to do, and you will know how good
and pleasing and perfect his will really is.

—Romans 12:2 NLT

I was fifteen the day I opened my yearbook and read, "Voted least likely to succeed—Kate McVeigh." Tears flowed as I cried out, "God, if You don't do something, I'm going to kill myself."

From the fifth grade, I had been in classes for slow learners. The other kids made fun of me, calling me "Sped" because I was enrolled in Special Education. I developed an overwhelming inferiority complex and imagined myself a hopeless loser.

Then one day I attended one of Kenneth Hagin's meetings. His message offered something completely new to me— hope. I was saved and filled with the Holy Spirit, and immediately a great weight lifted off my shoulders. Depression and fear, which had been my constant companions, were gone. The thoughts of suicide—gone.

Soon I learned about claiming favor in every area of life. I began to see who God says I am in the Word and refused to think about myself in any other way. It wasn't long before people took notice.

My teachers were shocked by the improvement in my academic performance. I was even voted "Most Valuable Player" on the basketball team, whereas before, my hands quivered so much from fear that I was rarely allowed to play.

God's Word is *powerful*. It literally transformed me from the inside out. His Word will transform you too.[12]

make **your** day count

Make your day count! Begin to claim God's favor over every area of your life today, and begin to see yourself being transformed by His Word.

A Life of Abundance

Gloria Copeland

God is able to make all grace (every favor and earthly blessing) come to you in abundance.

—2 Corinthians 9:8 AMP

Have you ever noticed that you never hear, "Oh my, I have more money than I need"? Such words sound ridiculous in a world ruled by lack, yet as children of God, that is what we *should* be saying!

Jesus said that we're *in* this world, but we're not *of* it. (John 17:15,16.) We belong to the kingdom of God, and it has no shortages. It has an abundant supply of every resource you will ever need.

Years ago when the only abundance Ken and I had was an abundance of needs, the Lord quickened the text verse to me. In the face of our impossible-looking situation, we chose to believe God's Word and began saying, "God is able to make every earthly blessing come to us in abundance!" We started speaking prosperity instead of lack, and we began obeying the promptings of the Holy Spirit where our finances were concerned. Miraculously, eleven months later, we were completely debt free.

Financially, we had been total failures, yet simply because we believed God and obeyed His Word, God was able to supply us not according to the shortages of this world, but according to His riches in glory. If you will dare to believe God's Word and begin speaking it instead of your circumstances, He'll do the same for you and abundance will be yours.[13]

make **your** day count

Make your day count! Write down the text verse, and throughout the day, speak its truth over your life, choosing to believe God's Word instead of any lack you may be experiencing.

time **saving** tips

Tips To Make Your Day Count

One fresh clove of garlic is equivalent to ⅛ teaspoon dried or powdered garlic or ½ teaspoon bottled or minced garlic.

To remove the papery skin from garlic cloves, try one of the following:

> Place the garlic cloves in the microwave for 15 seconds.

> Press the cloves firmly with the handle of a knife.

Place the cloves in very hot water for a couple of minutes before peeling.

Store peeled cloves in vegetable or olive oil in a jar in the refrigerator. They won't dry out, and the oil will be flavored for use in salad dressings and stir-frying.[14]

To get rid of garlic and onion smell on your hands, wash your hands as always. Then rub the "smelly" parts of your hands on a chrome faucet. The metal will absorb the odor!

easy **recipes**

Sour Cream Potato Salad[15]

Gloria Copeland

1/3 cup Italian salad dressing
6 cups (7 medium) potatoes, cooked in jackets, peeled, sliced
3/4 cup sliced celery
1/3 cup sliced green onion
4 hard-cooked eggs
1 cup mayonnaise or salad dressing
1/2 cup dairy sour cream
1/2 tsp. prepared horseradish mustard
Celery seed
Salt

Pour Italian dressing over warm potatoes.
Chill 2 hours.
Add celery and onion.
Chop egg whites; add. Sieve yolks.
Mix with mayonnaise, sour cream, and mustard.
Fold into salad.
Add salt and celery seed to taste.
Chill 2 hours.
Makes 8 servings.

More Than a New Year's Resolution

Marty Copeland

If the Son sets you free, you will be free indeed.

—John 8:36

A New Year's resolution promises gain, but lacks the substance to produce it. Any resolution that tries to bring about a transformation by fleshly effort instead of by the power of God sets you up for failure. True change and total victory occur only when we exercise our faith in the transforming power of God.

For over half my life, I was in bondage to overeating. I was obsessed with diets and exercise. I lost close to a total of seven hundred pounds through years of gaining then losing weight. Today, I'm totally, 100 percent free and experiencing the joy that comes with that freedom.

In theory, resolutions *sound* good, but they are just carnal methods that play right into Satan's deceptive strategy to keep us frustrated and failing until finally we lose all hope of ever being free. There is a way out; however, you will need to make a quality decision to put your hope and faith in God.

As you continue in the Word, trusting God to conform you to the image of His Son, that burden-removing, yoke-destroying power of Jesus the Anointed One and His anointing will set you free from the bondage of weight and the weight of bondage. You can confidently put your hope and trust in Him because when the Son makes you free, you are free indeed![16]

make **your** day count

Make your day count! Today, submit any areas of
bondage to the Lord and His yoke-destroying anointing.
Trust that He is transforming you even when you
don't see change. The Son will set you free!

How To Behave in a Cave

Cathy Duplantis

[Jesus said], In the world ye shall have tribulation:
but be of good cheer; I have overcome the world.

—John 16:33 KJV

The devil sends all kinds of tribulation to try to make you run and hide in a cave. Perhaps fear, discouragement, failure, or disappointment has driven you there. If so, be of good cheer!

No matter what has chased you into a cave, it hasn't come to stay. It *will* pass away. Jesus said, "Heaven and earth shall pass away, but my words shall not pass away" (Matt. 24:35 KJV). You can declare about anything that has come against you, "That thing is in the earth, and it's going to pass away! God's Word is going to dominate my situation, because it will *never* pass away!"

David of the Old Testament found himself in a cave situation. King Saul had become terribly jealous of David's success and popularity after the shepherd boy slew Goliath—so jealous, in fact, that Saul sent his army to kill David. David escaped to the cave Adullam.

Psalm 57 is an account of David's thoughts during his time there, and we can benefit from five things he learned that led him out. He learned to: 1) take refuge in God,

2) cry out to God, 3) declare God's promises, 4) expect victory, and 5) give praise to his God.

If you find yourself in a cave today, don't lose heart. Follow David's example and emerge the victor![17]

make **your** day count

Make your day count! Are you in a "cave"?
If so, begin following David's example today.
Each step will bring you closer to your way of escape.

Let Go of Your Problems

Patricia Salem

Let him have all your worries and cares,
for he is always thinking about you and
watching everything that concerns you.

—1 Peter 5:7 TLB

Negative situations are always going to come against us, and we can either go crazy or go to God and say, "Father, in myself I can't handle this problem, but You can." When you have the Word of God and start praying, He comes on the scene.

God has never forsaken or forgotten me, and although He doesn't always give me the answer *I'm* looking for, His answer always brings peace.

Sometimes we have to tell God about a problem and then drop it. When my husband died, I was living in Michigan and getting ready to move to Florida. There were many business affairs to settle, and a lot of greedy people came against me.

I said, "Lord, I can't handle this on my own. I will not move with bitterness in my heart toward anyone, and I want You to tell me how to handle this."

The Lord said, *Dig a burial plot six feet deep in your mind. Then take all these offenses, dump them into that hole, and cover them with dirt. Finally, plant beautiful flowers over that spot and never remember those offenses again. And as you forgive others, I will never remember your offenses again.*

When we let go of our problems and look to God for the answer, He will help us move forward in our lives.[18]

make **your** day count

Make your day count! Are you facing an issue that you can't handle alone?
Take it to God today, asking for His wisdom.
Then let go of that care and receive His guidance and peace.

time **saving** tips

Table-Etiquette Tips

Colleen Rickenbacher[19]

The following are helpful table-etiquette tips:

Hold cutlery properly; don't wave it around. Once you pick up a piece of silverware, it should never touch the table again.

Place the napkin over your lap as soon as you are seated. When you leave, do not fold the napkin. Lay it loosely to the left of your plate.

Never chew with your mouth open or talk with your mouth full of food.

Sit up straight; keep elbows off the table. If you have any doubt about your hands, put them in your lap.

Put butter on your plate. Break off one bite-sized piece of bread at a time, buttering each piece just before you eat it.

Don't pick your teeth or put on lipstick at the table.

Keep everything off the table unless it is part of the meal. This includes eyeglasses, hats, gloves, and briefcases.

Patricia Salem's Coleslaw[20]

Patricia Salem

1 small head cabbage, finely chopped or grated
2 carrots, chopped fine
1 small green or sweet red bell pepper, seeded, chopped fine
2 green onions, chopped fine

Dressing:
1 cup salad dressing
½ cup milk
1 Tbsp. sugar
Salt and pepper to taste

In a bowl, mix salad dressing, milk, sugar, salt, and pepper.
Add cabbage, carrots, pepper, onion, and mix well.
Cover with foil, and let stand several hours or overnight.

Intimacy in Marriage Starts with Friendship

Brenda Timberlake-White

Greater love has no one than this,
that he lay down his life for his friends.
—John 15:13

Most couples think they are friends before they marry but somehow "lose" their friendship after the wedding. Yet the person you are married to should be the best and most intimate friend you have!

If your marriage lacks intimacy, you may need to backtrack. A house must be built upon a strong foundation that has had time to settle in order for it to be sturdy. Likewise, intimacy doesn't happen overnight. It is not love at first sight. You can have the "hots" for someone you see for the first time, but you cannot love that person because you do not know him or her. Intimacy has to be developed over many hours of conversing; it involves knowing the heart of the person.

Intimacy in marriage is partly sexual, but it involves much more. It is a close relationship between two people who deeply love and appreciate one another, regardless of shortcomings and failures. It loves like Jesus loves, laying its life down for its friend, loving without limit. It is totally accepting and forgiving. An intimate friend loves out of commitment, not on condition.

Developing intimacy in marriage takes a lot of hard work, but there's nothing that can compare to being married to your best friend. It's a little bit of heaven, right here on earth—well worth the investment.[21]

make **your** day count

Make your day count! If you are married, make a date with your spouse to just talk. Treat your spouse as you would a friend you are trying to get to know better.

The Spirit of Jezebel Unmasked

Lindsay Roberts

These things have I written unto you
concerning them that seduce you.

—1 John 2:26 KJV

When most of us hear the name *Jezebel*, we think of someone who tries to steal another woman's husband. We think of the spirit of Jezebel as a woman because the first time this spirit manifested in the Bible was *through* a woman, Queen Jezebel. (1 Kings 16-19.)

The spirit of Jezebel is not a person, but a spirit—with an agenda to seduce you from your relationship with God and what He has called you to do. It can use money, power, position, or even the church in the form of religion to tear you away from God.

Let me give you an agenda of five things the spirit of Jezebel uses to try to destroy you.

1. Fear. A spirit that comes to torment, control, and paralyze you.

2. Discouragement. When you should be rejoicing, you wish you'd never been born. (1 Kings 19:4.)

3. Confusion. You don't know whether you're coming or going.

4. Self-doubt. You doubt your self-worth, causing you to retreat, which opens the door for terror.

5. Terror.

If any of these things are controlling you, ask God to help you. Repent of anything you may need to, because repentance leads to restoration. And there is good news: Everything Jesus did on the cross was to restore you.[22]

make **your** day count

Make your day count! Declare, "I refuse to be seduced
by the spirit of Jezebel and live in fear, discouragement,
confusion, self-doubt, or terror. I focus on the Word of God.
Whatever God says is mine, I receive by faith in Jesus' name!"

Nothing Is Too Little for God

Patricia Salem

Ask and you will receive, and your joy will be complete.
—John 16:24

I have always believed God for miracles—both big and small. Late one afternoon, I needed to drop something off that had to be in the mail that day. Then I realized I didn't have a stamp—and the post office was closing soon.

My car was parked in the huge parking lot at the Mabee Center on the campus of Oral Roberts University. As I drove across the lot to our TV studio, I prayed, "Lord, You know Lindsay doesn't like for me to drive and get out of my car at night, and the post office is about to close. Lord, I really need a stamp. Could You just get me *one?*"

The Mabee Center parking lot has *thousands* of parking spaces, and it had been a windy day. But as I parked my car and started to put my foot on the ground, right by my toe was *one single postage stamp!*

I began to sob. I said, "Lord, why do You always provide so well for me?"

And the Lord replied, *You always ask.*

Don't be afraid to ask God for what you need, big or small. It gives God pleasure to give to His children, even if it is something as small as a postage stamp![23]

make **your** day count

Make your day count! Today, ask God for all the little needs that come your way. And be sure to thank Him when He answers.

Time-Saving Airline Tips

Put your identification in a place where you can access it quickly. You will have to show it several times.

Do not pack or bring prohibited items to the airport. Visit www.tsa.gov for a complete list.

Leave gifts unwrapped. They may be opened for inspection.

Avoid wearing clothing, jewelry, and accessories that contain metal, because they may set off the alarm on a metal detector. Put any necessary metal in your carry-on bag. This includes jewelry, loose change, keys, cell phones, pagers, and PDAs.

Put all undeveloped film and cameras with film in your carry-on baggage. Checked-baggage screening equipment will damage undeveloped film.

Carry-on baggage is limited to one carry-on bag plus one personal item. Personal items include laptops, purses, small backpacks, briefcases, and camera cases.

Place identification tags in and on all of your baggage, including your laptop computer.[24]

easy **recipes**

Beef Stew [25]

Patricia Salem

2 lbs. stew meat, remove all fat, cut into 2" pieces
1 Tbsp. canola oil
1 package dried onion soup mix
2 cups water
1 large can whole tomatoes
6 carrots, peeled and cut into 2" chunks
3 small onions, cut into quarters
6 small potatoes, peeled

Remove all fat from meat and cube into 1½" to 2" pieces.

Brown the meat in canola oil on medium heat until all meat is completely browned.

Remove from heat and drain well.

Stir in 1 package dried onion soup mix and water. Stir and simmer for about 1½ hours or until meat is beginning to get tender.

Add 1 large can whole tomatoes, carrots, onions, and potatoes and continue simmering until vegetables are cooked.

This is nice served with sourdough bread and a green salad.

Who Are You?

Billye Brim

If anyone is in Christ, he is a new creation;
the old has gone, the new has come!
—2 Corinthians 5:17

The most important thing we have to know when we pray is who we are in Christ. And we know that by meditating on the Word of God.

Think about how Jesus came to see Himself as the Savior. He was the Son of God, but He was human too, just like we are. He came to earth as a baby who had to be taught to walk and talk. He also had to be taught the things of God, just like you and I do.

Jesus had to study God's Word to see what the prophets of old had said about Him. We know He studied even as a child because in Luke 2:47, at age twelve, Jesus was found teaching the elders in the temple. Everyone was astonished at His understanding. *Jesus saw who He was when He meditated on the Scriptures,* and this is exactly how we will see who we are in Him! You're not a weak sinner saved by grace. You are the temple of the living God. As such, take your place in Christ and walk in the authority that is yours.[26]

make **your** day count

Find one verse, such as the text verse, that tells you
who you are in Christ. Throughout the day today,
see yourself in light of that verse and take your place in Him.

Don't Get Stressed Out, Stand Still!

Lindsay Roberts

Fear ye not, stand still, and see the salvation of the LORD.
—Exodus 14:13 KJV

Are you so overwhelmed by everything you need to accomplish that you feel as though you might crack? I understand what it's like to be stressed. It's difficult to find balance in our lives with our hectic schedules and multitude of responsibilities.

Fear is a major cause of stress, yet there are many places in the Bible where God tells us to "fear not." When we "fear not," we are able to step outside the realm of being panic-stricken by circumstances. Then we are to "stand still."

Have you ever tried to make sense to a person who is running around all stressed out? In contrast, if you will stand still and get into an atmosphere of faith, you will "see the salvation of the Lord."

When I looked up this Scripture in the original text, I found that it means, "One who comes from outside to bring help." When you're in the middle of a stressful situation, the problems are often all you can see. Of course, if you were in the middle of a fire, the situation would look really bad to you. But if you were *outside* the fire, you would be able to handle it more rationally. God deals with your circumstances from outside the stress, so step outside with Him. He has the solution you need![27]

make **your** day count

Make a conscious effort to "step out of" your circumstances today. Stand still with God outside those circumstances, and watch as He saves the day.

How We Learned To Live by Faith

Gloria Copeland

We live by faith, not by sight.
—2 Corinthians 5:7

Over thirty-five years ago, Ken and I began living by faith. We were living in Tulsa and had absolutely nothing! At thirty, Ken was Oral Roberts University's oldest freshman as well as a copilot for Oral Roberts.

One day Ken came home proclaiming, "We are going to become Oral Roberts' partners and send ten dollars a month as seed-faith offerings!"

"Where in the world will we get ten dollars?" I asked.

I hadn't heard the faith sermons Ken had been hearing, and I didn't have the supernatural revelations that he had been receiving. But as we began to sow our seed, we began to increase. Unexpected money began to come our way. We had also begun to tithe. The more we went after the Word of God, the more God manifested Himself. He wants to increase us, and that requires us to walk by faith.

The only way faith comes is by hearing, believing, and acting on God's Word. Faith sees ahead as though it were today. It sees the answer in the Word of God.

We don't have to pray for grocery money anymore, but we still have to study God's Word and believe Him to help us fulfill His call. We will always have to live by faith, but after thirty-five years of doing so, we wouldn't want to live any other way.[28]

make **your** day count

Think of a ministry that has been feeding you
spiritual food and send a seed-faith gift today.
Then expect the financial harvest you need!

time **saving** tips

Tips To Make Your Day Count

To remove blood stains, treat the spot with hydrogen peroxide, then launder as usual. (Test inconspicuous area first.)

To remove ballpoint pen ink, saturate material with an alcohol-based hair spray. The alcohol content in the hair spray will break up the ink. Be sure to place an absorbent paper towel or rag under the stain to catch the excess. You then need to blot the stain with a rag. Repeat the process until the stain is removed, then launder as usual. (Test on an inconspicuous area first, or consult with a professional dry cleaner.)

To remove candle wax or chewing gum, put the item in the freezer until the wax is hardened. Then chip it off.[29]

$100 Cake[30]

Gloria Copeland

2 ½ cups sugar
1 cup shortening or 2 sticks butter or margarine
5 eggs, separated
1 cup buttermilk
3 cups cake flour
5 Tbsp. strong coffee
4 Tbsp. cocoa, rounded
1 pinch salt
1 tsp. soda
2 tsp. vanilla

Cream butter and sugar thoroughly. Sift dry ingredients
together. Beat egg whites and yolks separately. Add yolks to
sugar and butter, mixing well. Add dry ingredients alter-
nately with liquids. Fold in well-beaten egg whites last. Bake
at 375° for 20-25 minutes or until done. Makes 3 layers.

Icing:
3 Tbsp. cocoa
½ cup butter (1 stick)
3 Tbsp. strong coffee (or more, to taste)
1 box powdered sugar
1 egg yolk
1 tsp. vanilla

Sift sugar with cocoa.
Cream butter; add sugar and cocoa mixture with liquids and
beat well with electric mixer.

Time for a Turnaround

Dodie Osteen

I turned away from God but I was sorry afterwards.
I kicked myself for my stupidity. I was thoroughly
ashamed of all I did in younger days.

—Jeremiah 31:19 TLB

Have you ever turned away from God? Were you sorry? Did you feel grieved in your heart because you knew that you had grieved God? Have you ever wanted to kick yourself for your stupidity? I have.

But God doesn't see us as stupid—He just sees us as learners. Although we make mistakes, He doesn't see us as failures, but as people who are seeking truth.

Sometimes we are thoroughly ashamed of all that we've done. Maybe you are ashamed of something you have done recently. If you are truly sorry, call out to God. Psalm 34:18 TLB says, "The Lord is close to those whose hearts are breaking; he rescues those who are humbly sorry for their sins." God will draw close; He will rescue you and forgive you.

After you have repented and received God's forgiveness, turn around. Take the right path. Proverbs 2:20,21 TLB says, "Follow the steps of the godly instead, and stay on the right path, for only good men enjoy life to the full."

When you choose the right path, you'll feel good in your heart, and you won't have to be concerned about grieving God. You'll make the Lord proud of you, and you will be able to enjoy life to the full.[31]

make **your** day count

If you have done something that you are ashamed of,
repent of that thing now. Don't go another minute carrying that burden.
Instead, run into your Father's arms and live today to the full.

Thrive, Don't Just Survive!

Cathy Duplantis

*He shall be like a tree planted by the rivers of water, that
bringeth forth his fruit in his season; his leaf also shall
not wither; and whatsoever he doeth shall prosper.*

—Psalm 1:3 KJV

After many years of trying to grow beautiful houseplants,
I have finally conceded that this is just not my season for it. I
really do care about them, but when I'm on the road ministering with Jesse, I don't even think about those plants. When
we return home and walk through the door, however, there
they are, begging for water. Once again, I try to revive them
from yet another near-death experience.

Do you feel like my houseplants, existing in "survival
mode"? Well, God doesn't want you just fighting for survival,
He wants you to *thrive! To thrive* means "to make steady
progress; prosper. To grow vigorously; flourish."[32] You were
created in God's image, and He made you to flourish!

Psalm 1 describes God's three-step plan for us to thrive.
If we (1) choose not to hang with the wrong crowd and
(2) crave God's Word and feed on it, we shall (3) live a long,
fruitful, prosperous life!

Cultivate relationships with people who have a strong
walk with God, people who won't drag you down. Crave and

feed on God's Word because it fills you with wisdom to thrive over challenges.

It may not come overnight, but if you will follow these principles, God has promised that you will flourish and bring forth much fruit. Now that's thriving. Decide to do it today![33]

make **your** day count

Call a friend whose walk with God inspires you and invite her
out for lunch. It will be a great investment in your friendship,
and it will provide a nourishing "meal" to feed your spirit and soul.

Establishing Your Priorities

Sharon Daugherty

Teach us to number our days and recognize how few
they are; help us to spend them as we should.

—Psalm 90:12 TLB

God's priorities should be what we seek in life. If we follow His plan, we'll walk with proper balance in all of our responsibilities. Establish what things are most important, then let everything else fall into its right place. I've found the following guidelines, in this order, to be helpful: time with God, time with husband, time with family, and time for ministry.

Wife and motherhood duties fall into order as we first submit our ways to God. Time with God is so vital. If we don't have time with Him, we won't be filled up to handle the day effectively. Spiritually speaking, we'll run out of patience, joy, peace, and self-control; and we'll miss God's leading in areas.

On the other hand, if we start our day with prayer and God's Word, we can put on the armor of God, our spirits will be filled with the fruit of the Holy Spirit, and our hearts will be sensitive to hear God's voice speaking to us.

Take time to read and study God's Word every day, even if it's only a few minutes. Don't let the devil talk you out of it. Remember, you are in a spiritual battle and you need to keep your guard up. Your time with God is your source of strength in life.[34]

make **your** day count

Set aside some time today to seek God, pray, and read His Word. Even if it is only fifteen minutes, any time you give God will help to fill you up, so you can effectively deal with the challenges of your day.

time **saving** tips

Keeping the Shower Clean

Betsy Williams

To make cleaning a shower easier and to keep it clean longer, hang a squeegee (which you can purchase at a discount store) and a hand towel in your shower stall. After showering, squeegee the walls. Then use the hand towel to dry any water that has collected along the caulk to prevent mildew from forming. Lastly, use the towel to dry all of the metal fixtures to prevent hard-water spots. This only takes a minute or two, but when it comes time to do a major cleaning, it'll be a snap.

easy **recipes**

Sausage Balls[35]

Sharon Daugherty

1 lb. sausage
1 lb. mild cheese, grated
3 cups Bisquick mix

Mix with hands; form into walnut-size balls.
Bake at 350° for 10 minutes.
For convenience, these may be frozen prior to baking.

The Four Stages of Friendship

Deborah Butler

Two are better than one, because they have
a good return for their work: If one falls down,
his friend can help him up.

—Ecclesiastes 4:9,10

Friends are a gift from God. But good friendships don't just happen; there is a process involved. I believe there are four stages of friendship: the acquaintance stage, the casual friendship, the close friendship, and the intimate friendship. Each of these stages must be handled correctly in order for the relationship to be godly. We need God's guidance throughout the process.

The acquaintance stage takes place when you first meet someone. An acquaintance becomes a casual friend when you spend time with the person, ask basic questions, and pray. We have the responsibility to ask God, "Why has this person crossed my path? Did You send this person?"

Once you have gone through the acquaintance and casual friendship stages with someone, you use the same standards for establishing a close friendship. Here you decide at what level the relationship should stay. If you desire to bring the person further into your life, then you move to the intimate friendship stage, which involves best friends and even marriage.

It is important that we teach our children this process also. After years of practice in establishing what type of relationship is or isn't right for them, it will help them in their dating relationships. It will even help them know when they've found the person whom they are to marry. Friends are a great blessing at every stage.[36]

make **your** day count

Call one of your intimate friends today to let him or her know how much you appreciate the friendship you share.

Steps Toward Receiving Your Healing

Lindsay Roberts

Jesus said, I tell you, whatever you ask for in prayer,
believe that you have received it, and it will be yours.

—Mark 11:24 NIV

Do you need healing? According to this verse, you can believe for and receive the healing you need!

First, you must believe when you pray. Notice that the verse doesn't say believe *after* you receive; it says believe *when* you pray, even if you haven't seen the manifestation of it yet.

Second, God is a rewarder. Hebrews 11:6 KJV says that God "is a rewarder of them that diligently seek him." What would God do as a rewarder? We know that sickness and disease cannot come from Him because Matthew 7:11 says He gives *good* gifts to His children. James 1:17 says that every *good* and *perfect* gift comes from Him.

Third, hold on to your faith. Luke 8 tells the story about a man named Jairus who asked Jesus to heal his daughter. As Jairus and Jesus were headed to his house, Jairus received word that his daughter had died. But Jesus said, "Don't be afraid; just believe, and she will be healed" (v. 50). Jairus made the decision to hold on to his faith, and Jesus raised his daughter from the dead.

Fourth, don't give up. Your miracle could be as close as your next breath. You don't want to miss it by giving up!

Finally, after you have prayed and asked, begin to praise God that the answer is on its way.[37]

make **your**
day count

Do you need healing in your body?
Review these five principles and act on them today.

Let Your Definite Request Be Made Known

Evelyn Roberts

Do not fret or have any anxiety about anything,
but in every circumstance…by prayer and petition
(definite requests) with thanksgiving, continue
to make your wants known to God.

—Philippians 4:6 AMP

With Oral Roberts, winning souls and getting people healed has always been the strongest cry of his heart, so when pastors asked him to continue his tent crusade in Dallas in 1948, he called me long distance. He said, "Evelyn, this meeting is wonderful. I don't see how I can close it in time to be home on Wednesday when the baby is expected."

I'm pretty sure that no one but Oral Roberts would do this, but he asked, "Honey, can you put off having the baby for a day or two? I could be home on Thursday. Let's agree in prayer that the baby won't arrive until then."

I didn't doubt that the Lord could answer this request. I had simply never asked Him to do anything like that before. But I said to Oral, "You'll be too tired on Thursday. As long as we're asking the Lord to change the time, let's set it for Friday before midnight. The Lord understands."

Sure enough, on Friday, November 12, at 11:20 P.M., Richard was born. The Lord answered our prayer so that Oral could stay and minister God's healing and salvation to the precious people in Dallas.[38]

make **your** day count

Think of something specific you want or need today,
and ask God for it, making your definite request known to Him.

time **saving** tips

Tips To Make Your Day Count

Save time and keep clutter to a minimum when preparing a meal. Simply hook one of the handles of a plastic bag to a knob on one of your kitchen drawers or cabinets. Or you can hook one handle over the side of a drawer and close the drawer. You can then clear debris into the bag as you go. When you're done, you can dispose of the rubbish with one trip to the trash bin.[39]

Banana Bread[40]

Evelyn Roberts

½ cup oil (4 Tbsp. margarine)
1½ cups sugar
2 eggs, well beaten
¼ tsp. salt
1½ cups sifted flour
1 tsp. baking soda
½ cup buttermilk
½ cup sour cream
3 to 4 ripe bananas, mashed
1 cup chopped pecans

Mix together first 8 ingredients.
Then add bananas and chopped pecans.
Grease and flour 2 loaf pans.
Bake at 350° for 45 minutes.

Everything but the Kitchen Sink

Patricia Salem

Be careful to obey all the law my servant Moses gave you;
do not turn from it to the right or to the left,
that you may be successful wherever you go.

—Joshua 1:7

My grandmother was an excellent cook. But it was always an adventure to eat her cooking because she was always adding extra ingredients that weren't part of the original recipe.

When I asked her to teach me how to make her apple pie recipe, she replied, "Use half Granny Smith and half Spy apples. Cut them up. Add some sugar, butter, and a little flour in layers. Then make a rich, buttery piecrust to go over the top and bake it."

That sounded like the complete recipe, but I knew there was more to it than that. Often she would go to the icebox where she might find some leftover peaches, which she would add. If it was in the icebox, it was going into the pie!

Grandma had a very successful "everything but the kitchen sink" approach to cooking. While that might work in the kitchen, it doesn't work when it comes to leading an overcoming Christian life. We must follow the "recipe" God has given us in His Word. It doesn't work to add our own ingredients or put our own twist on God's Word.

But if you will follow the guidelines established in His Word, "blessings shall come upon you and overtake you, because you obey the voice of the LORD your God" (Deut. 28:2 NKJV)![41]

make **your** day count

Commit to live according to God's Word. If there are areas where you are not doing things His way, ask Him to help you make the necessary adjustments, so His blessings can overtake you.

How To Meditate on the Word

Billye Brim

My eyes stay open through the watches of the night,
that I may meditate on your promises.
—Psalm 119:148

The whole book of Ephesians is wonderful for meditation. It tells us who we are in Christ. I want to share an example of a prayer and meditation—based on Ephesians 1:17—that I pray and say every day. First, I pray it over those in authority, both government and spiritual leaders. Then I pray it over myself. You can also pray this over your loved ones.

"I keep asking that the God of our Lord Jesus Christ, the glorious Father, may give you the Spirit of wisdom and revelation, so that you may know him better" (Eph. 1:17). I pray through verse 23 and then go over to Ephesians 2, verses 1, 5, and 6.

First, I pray the prayer part. Then I meditate on my position in Christ. God has raised me up together with Christ, and I am seated with Him in the heavenlies—far above all principality, and power, and might, and dominion, and every name that is named! How could we ever feel depressed when we are so seated and blessed!

Meditating on God's Word is not difficult. It just requires a little time and effort on your part. But if you will commit to do it, God's Word will not return void. It will transform your life.[42]

make **your** day count

Pray the prayers in Ephesians 1 and 2,
and meditate on the wonderful promises that
are yours because of your new life in Christ.

Protected by the Blood of Jesus

Kellie Copeland Kutz

They overcame him by the blood of the
Lamb and by the word of their testimony.

—Revelation 12:11

Shortly after my cousin Nikki, an on-fire-for-God believer, was killed in an accident involving a drunk driver, I began to seek the Lord to find out how we could make sure this never happened again. That very week, I heard Billye Brim teach on the blood of Jesus, stressing, "We have to plead the blood of Jesus over our families every morning and every night."

As I began to study the Word on the subject, I read about God supernaturally protecting the Israelites from the plagues sent against Pharaoh and his people for refusing to let God's people go. In Exodus 12, God instituted the Passover to protect the Israelites from the final judgment on the Egyptians: the death of every firstborn son.

In Exodus 12:7 KJV, God instructed the Israelites to "take of the blood, and strike it on the two side posts and on the upper doorpost of the houses." Those who obeyed were pro-tected behind the blood and escaped death. Today, we can apply the blood of Jesus to the "doorposts" of our lives by speaking words of faith.

God is offering us assurance that our loved ones will be protected. We do this by walking in the light of the Word and appropriating His promise of protection through the blood of Jesus.[43]

make **your** day count

Present yourself and those you love to the Lord today, striking the doorposts of your lives with the blood of Jesus by faith.

Walking in the Spirit

Sharon Daugherty

Walk in the Spirit, and you shall not
fulfill the lust of the flesh.

—Galatians 5:16 NKJV

When I began my walk with the Lord, I did not know what "walking in the Spirit" meant. This verse says that it means not walking according to the dictates of the flesh. Rather, we are to be controlled by the Spirit within.

When you receive Jesus into your heart, your old way of life ceases to exist and a new life begins. You receive the Spirit of God into your heart, and your own spirit is born again. You become a new person inside.

But *living* in the Spirit and *walking* in the Spirit are two different things. Galatians 5:25 NKJV states, "If we live in the Spirit, let us also walk in the Spirit." Children born into a family learn to walk, or conduct themselves, like their parents. Even though they are born into the family, walking does not come automatically. It takes time and effort learning to walk. Likewise, you can be born into God's family, but not yet walk like our Father. When you seek to please God, you'll learn His walk and His talk. As time goes by, it will become more and more your natural inclination to walk and talk like Him.

First John 2:6 AMP says, "Whoever says he abides in Him ought...to walk and conduct himself in the same way in which He walked and conducted Himself." It is a continual growing process, but once you understand that it isn't you living your life anymore, but Jesus in you, with you yielding to Him, then you will be "walking in the Spirit."[44]

make **your** day count

In every situation you face today, ask, "What would Jesus do?" Then walk in the Spirit by yielding to Him and His way of doing things.

time **saving** tips

Start with "A-priority" tasks; is what you're doing the best use of your time?

Fight procrastination; do it now if it's important.

Subdivide large tasks into smaller, easy to accomplish segments.

Establish a quiet time.

Find a hideaway, such as a library.

Learn to say no when you have something important to do.

Learn to delegate.

Accumulate similar tasks and do them all at one time.

Throw away junk mail. Try to handle paper only once.

Avoid perfectionism.

Avoid over-commitment and over-scheduling.

Set time limits.

Concentrate on what you are doing.

Use big blocks of time for big jobs.

Think the job through before acting.

Finish as you go; get it right the first time.[45]

Cheezy Green Beans[46]

Sharon Daugherty

2 cans French-cut green beans
Bacon drippings
Cracker crumbs

Cheese sauce:
1 cup mushrooms
1/4 stick margarine
1 cup milk
1/4 lb. Velveeta cheese, grated
1 heaping tsp. flour
1 tsp. Worcestershire sauce
1/4 cup chopped nuts

Heat first 5 cheese sauce ingredients until smooth.

Add Worcestershire sauce and chopped nuts.

Add cheese sauce to 2 cans French-cut green beans that have been seasoned with bacon drippings.

Cover with buttered crumbs and bake at 350° for 30 minutes.

The Body/Finance Connection

Marty Copeland

Present your bodies a living sacrifice, holy, acceptable
to God, which is your reasonable service.
—Romans 12:1 NKJV

The prosperity of your body is as much a part of your covenant as the prosperity of your finances. Health and wealth are spiritually linked. It's what I call the body/finance connection.

One afternoon, as I was praying for people's deliverance from food addiction, the Lord dropped these words into my heart: *Trying to lose weight without presenting your body as a living sacrifice is like trying to prosper financially without tithing.* It just won't work.

God's Word says there are three things that belong to God: your spirit, your body, and your tithe. First Corinthians 6:19,20 states that your body is the temple of the Holy Spirit and you are not your own. You were bought with a price.

Why does God ever ask anything of us? So He can get something to us. Submitting your spirit to the lordship of Jesus gives you eternal life. Submitting your tithes and offerings to God gives you prosperity. As you submit your body to God as a living sacrifice, you are giving your firstfruits, so all the rest will be blessed. He will get involved in your eating habits; He will get involved in your weight loss.

Health and prosperity are part of your covenant. Grab hold of them! You've got the right—the covenant right![47]

make **your** day count

Say, "God lives inside me. I have my body because of God. It's not my own. I've been bought with a price. Father, I submit my body to You as a living sacrifice. Thank You for blessing it."

When Someone's Baggage Influences Your World

Lindsay Roberts

Let's please the other fellow, not ourselves, and do what is for his good and thus build him up in the Lord.

—Romans 15:2 TLB

Most of us encounter at least one or two difficult people who seem to rip our peace right out from under us the minute they walk through the door. What do you do when that happens—especially when it's someone close to you?

The Bible tells us that God's love is the key. It's important to remember that the problem isn't the person who is trying to steal your peace. Ephesians 6:12 says, "Our struggle is not against flesh and blood, but against the rulers, against the authorities, against the powers of this dark world and against the spiritual forces of evil in the heavenly realms."

We all know good people with bad baggage. I believe that the spirit of fear is often behind the anxiety and torment people carry in their lives. When their baggage begins to influence your world, your responsibility is to be like God. God is love, so you are to demonstrate the love of God to them.

We must approach these people with love, remembering that the love of God can remove that junk out of their lives.

God will empower you to be patient and kind as you yield yourself to Him. Who knows, you may be just the one God wants to use to bring healing and wholeness to that person.[48]

make **your** day count

Seek out someone whose "baggage" is a challenge to you and purposely bless the person with God's love today.

Tune in Again Tomorrow!

Taffi L. Dollar

*Listen to me; blessed are those who keep my ways...Blessed
is the man who listens to me, watching daily at my doors.*
—Proverbs 8:32,34

Learning to hear God's voice isn't a one-time event. It requires daily communication with Him. I believe we are to pursue hearing His voice as if our very survival depended on it. John 5:25 KJV says, "The hour is coming, and now is, when the dead shall hear the voice of the Son of God: and they that hear shall live."

When Jesus says that these "shall live," He's not talking about barely making it from one day to the next. He's talking about developing intimate communication with God.

God has created you to accomplish great things, but it's going to take hearing from Him to be able to do them. The good news is that *you were made to hear God's voice!* Deuteronomy 4:36 KJV says, "Out of heaven he made thee to hear his voice, that he might instruct thee." Just as children must hear the voice of their mother so that she can instruct and encourage them, you were made to hear your Father's voice.

God is speaking all the time. It's up to us to tune in with our spiritual ears to hear what He is saying through His

Word. He wants us to hear Him so that He can divinely direct us. Determine today to hear God's voice, and as He speaks, obey.[49]

make your day count

Claim Psalm 85:8 as your own by saying,
"I will hear what God the LORD will speak to me today!"
Then tune in and listen.

Say What?

Patricia Salem

The tongue has the power of life and death,
and those who love it will eat its fruit.
—Proverbs 18:21

The words we speak are powerful. We read in James 3:8 that "no man can tame the tongue. It is a restless evil, full of deadly poison." But I know from personal experience that God can help you tame your tongue if you ask Him.

When I was growing up, my father wasn't a Christian, and he cursed a lot. I thought that was just the way people talked, so I picked it up and began cursing too.

One day after I had accepted Christ, I was driving in the car with my children, who were small at the time, and I used my precious Lord's name in vain. I felt so terrible that my children had heard me. When we got home, I knelt on my knees and said, "Lord, I'd rather not have a tongue in my head than to use Your wonderful name in vain. I give my tongue to You and ask You to please change me."

That was in the late 1950s, and from that time to this, I have never cursed or used God's name in vain again. I wasn't capable of taming my tongue by myself, but when I submitted it to God and genuinely asked for His help, He changed me. He'll do no less for you![50]

make **your** day count

Pray, "Father, I want my words to be words of life.
I submit my tongue to You today and ask You to help me tame it. Amen."

time **saving** tips

Uses for Rubbing Alcohol

Betsy Williams

 To clean telephones, moisten a cotton ball or Q-Tip with rubbing alcohol and wipe clean. (Be careful not to allow alcohol to drip into crevices.)

 Rubbing alcohol also works to remove adhesive residue (from price tags or other labels) on glass, plastic, and china. (It is always a good idea to test an inconspicuous area first.) Apply with cotton and "thumb roll" the adhesive into balls and remove.[51]

Caramel Corn[52]

Patricia Salem

4 to 6 quarts popped popcorn

2 cups brown sugar

1 cup margarine

1 cup light corn syrup

$\frac{1}{2}$ tsp. cream of tartar

$\frac{1}{2}$ tsp. baking soda

Pop the corn according to package directions and set aside in a large bowl.

In a heavy saucepan, add sugar, margarine, and corn syrup and bring to a boil.

Cook 5 minutes on medium heat, stirring constantly. (Make sure it keeps boiling.)

Remove from heat. Add cream of tartar, soda. Mix well with popped corn.

Put on cooking sheet and bake at 200° for 1 hour.

This is a treat for my grandchildren. It makes a large batch, but we usually don't store it. You can, however, put it in Tupperware for several days. It does store well.

Restoring the Lost Child in You

Joyce Meyer

He refreshes and restores my life (my self).
—Psalm 23:3 AMP

God is in the restoration business. "Restore" means to bring back into existence or to an original state. God desires to restore the "lost child" in us—those childlike qualities we have lost by being forced to grow up too quickly or because of various negative circumstances.

Satan is out to destroy children, and God is out to protect them. Satan tried to kill both Moses and Jesus when they were babies. In sharp contrast, Matthew 19:13,14 says that Jesus rebuked the disciples for preventing the children from coming to Him. He also said that unless we become like children, we cannot inherit the kingdom of God. (Matt. 18:3.) We are to take on a free, lighthearted nature—to become loving, forgiving, trusting, and carefree.

Because of the loss of childlikeness, many adults are dealing with tremendous emotional problems that are damaging their relationship with God, themselves, and others. But in John 10:10 AMP, Jesus said that He came that we may have and enjoy life.

In order for the child in you to be restored, you must lean on God continuously for everything you need. I encourage you to look for the humor in things and to relax, trust God, and take Him at His Word. Over time the lost child in you will be found and restored.[53]

make your day count

Think of one childlike quality you have lost,
and ask God to begin restoring it today.

God Has a Place for You

Gloria Copeland

He brought us to this place and gave us this land,
a land flowing with milk and honey.

—Deuteronomy 26:9

God has a plan for each of us, but did you know that He also has a physical place for us? When God created Adam and Eve, He made a place for them in the Garden. When He established the children of Israel as a people, He gave them the Promised Land.

I believe God has a physical place for us, but to receive it we are to diligently seek Him and His way of doing things. When we seek after God, we find His wisdom, we run into His goodness, and we open the door for the kingdom of heaven to be manifested, so we can live life supernaturally.

We don't have to live like the world lives. We have a Father in heaven who is in control, and He wants us to be like Him. That's why He gave Adam dominion over all things. Then God gave him instructions on how to live in the Garden.

Everything was perfect, nothing missing, nothing broken, until Adam and Eve failed to follow the wisdom of God for their lives and disobeyed Him. As a result, they lost their Garden.

God has a place of blessing for you, and I believe that if you'll stay connected to Him and follow His wisdom, your "place" will continually increase. You can't follow the wisdom of God and not increase.[54]

make **your** day count

Are you in the place that God has for you? If so, thank Him for it. If not, receive your "place" by faith and stay expectant.

God's Strength for Your Weakness

Dr. Patricia D. Bailey

The Lord said to Paul, "...my power is made perfect in weakness." Therefore I will boast all the more gladly about my weaknesses, so that Christ's power may rest on me.

—2 Corinthians 12:9

God has orchestrated a unique destiny for each of us— one that will exceed our greatest expectations, one that He wants to help us fulfill. But some feel trapped by behavior patterns. Others feel limited by personality traits. Some hide behind their challenges, without attempting to excel beyond them. Others in their own strength create the type of future they think they want, only to discover it isn't as fulfilling as they had expected.

These people have found they cannot transform themselves. Self-help may have provided a degree of success, but instead of depending on God, they have relied on themselves. It's *supposed* to be about depending on Jesus, so He can turn our weaknesses into strengths!

Above all, God wants our hearts. He wants *you.* Our part is to cooperate with Him by yielding to Him, so He can make the finishing touches on our rough edges. We do this by building an intimate relationship with Him—learning who God is, what He can and wants to do for us, and how to let Him work with us and for us. This takes time, as does any relationship, and it is a process of growing and maturing spiritually. But the investment will pay off as you fulfill God's perfect plan for your life.[55]

make **your** day count

Talk to God about your areas of weakness, and
ask Him to help you yield to Him, so He can turn
your greatest weakness into your greatest strength.

time **saving** tips

Car Tips for Snowy and Icy Weather

To keep windshields frost free, mix three parts vinegar to one part water and coat the windows with this solution. This vinegar and water combination will keep windshields ice and frost free.

Or, cover your windshield with rubber mats before you go to bed. The next morning when you pull them off, you will have ice-free windows.

When your windshield wiper blades get grungy, clean them with rubbing alcohol. You'll get more than just clean wipers—you'll also prevent ice from forming on the blades.

In the winter when condensation forms on the inside of your car windows, turn on the air-conditioning along with the heat. Your windows should clear up in no time.

If the locks on your car doors become frozen, use a hair dryer to melt the ice.[56]

Nanny's Sweet Potatoes

Julie Lechlider

Ingredients:

4-6 medium sweet potatoes

1 ½ sticks butter or margarine

2 cups brown sugar

Directions:

Peel sweet potatoes.

Cut potatoes into quarters.

Boil cut potatoes in water until they are tender. Drain.

Melt butter in a skillet.

Add the sweet potatoes to the butter and turn them once to coat.

Pour brown sugar on top and let it melt down into the potatoes and butter.

Cook over low heat until syrup forms.

*Note: You may need to add a little more brown sugar to make more syrup depending on how many potatoes are used. You may also add pancake syrup.

An Ambassador of Love

Terri Copeland Pearsons

God has given us the privilege of urging everyone to
come into his favor and be reconciled to him.

—2 Corinthians 5:18 TLB

You have been reconciled to God! And since you are born of His nature and love, it should be in you to take the message of reconciliation to those around you—to draw them close and love them.

Some might say, "Well, I couldn't possibly get close to *those* people! They're living in gross sin!"

Well, don't beat them with your judgment stick or try to punish them for their sin. Jesus already took the punishment for them! When we're tempted to be harsh or critical, we should ask ourselves, "Is this how Jesus would speak to this person? Is this the tone of voice He would use?"

Let God show you how to be loving to those people who give you the hardest time. He'll give you the power to do something nice for them. They will probably be ugly again, but the power of love will enable you to rise above it and it won't matter. What will matter, however, is that something eternal will have happened. The very love and presence of Almighty God will have come on the scene. And that love can do things that nothing else can do.

You can have the same awesome impact on your world that Jesus had. Love breaks chains. Heals wounds. Brings people together. Love makes the impossible possible, because love never fails.[57]

make **your** day count

When your path crosses that of someone who
is difficult to love today, sow a seed of love.
Water that seed tomorrow, then watch as your seed begins to grow.

Breaking Destructive Soul Ties

Lindsay Roberts

Stand fast therefore in the liberty wherewith
Christ hath made us free, and be not entangled
again with the yoke of bondage.
—Galatians 5:1 KJV

God has given each of us a spirit and a soul. Your spirit is the part of you that will live forever, even after it leaves your body. Your soul includes your mind, will, emotions, and decision-making processes. God designed the spirit to rule over the soul.

When it comes to the close relationships in your life, you knit your soul to another person's as a relationship grows. You develop a *soul tie* to that person. The danger comes when you knit yourself to someone who is not allowing the Spirit of God to lead them, someone who can pull down your soul so much that they eventually pull down your spirit. *That's a destructive soul tie.*

Perhaps you have left a bad or even abusive relationship, thinking that would end your connection with that person. But until you ask God to help you break that destructive soul tie, that relationship may still be influencing your other relationships and decisions.

God can create a "clean slate" in your soul, freeing you to begin again. Ask God to break any destructive soul ties you have. Then begin renewing your mind with the Word of God. Let the washing of God's Word begin to transform your life as you allow God to speak to your spirit and lead you into new and healthy relationships in Him.[58]

make **your** day count

If you are dealing with a destructive soul tie,
break the power of it right now in Jesus' name.
Determine that only God's thoughts will influence you today.

An Abundance of Peace

Marilyn Hickey

Grace and peace be yours in abundance through
the knowledge of God and of Jesus our Lord.
—2 Peter 1:2

When I was twenty-one years old, my father had a nervous breakdown. His personality changed tremendously. He would drink heavily and say cruel, terrible things. My brother and I were miserable; but my Spirit-filled mother experienced a tremendous peace. No one could understand it.

When my father turned himself in to a psychiatric center, the doctors tried to blame his sickness on my mother's religion. But she said, "No, my 'religion' didn't bring him here; but my 'religion' will take him out." And it did—her peace and faith in Jesus Christ finally rescued my father.

We live in a day when everyone wants peace. They want it so desperately, yet very few have real peace. The reason there is so little peace is because there is so little knowledge of God and so few people who have really made Jesus the Lord of their lives.

The more we make Jesus the Lord over our circumstances, desires, emotions, and decisions, the more we will find peace that is absolutely multiplied back to us. Saturate yourself with the peace of God's Word.[59]

make **your** day count

Meditate on the fact that Jesus is your Prince of Peace today.
The more you know Him in that way,
the more peace will be multiplied to you.

God's Good Plan for You

Evelyn Roberts

"I know the plans I have for you," declares the LORD,
"plans to prosper you and not to harm you,
plans to give you hope and a future."
—Jeremiah 29:11

I believe that each of us has a unique calling from our Creator and that He's given us the individual gifts and abilities needed to fulfill that call. Isn't it freeing to know that you don't have to be like someone else! God made you who you are and chose you for your particular calling.

Before I married Oral, I wanted to be a missionary. And although God never called me to do that, I still struggled with the idea after we married. It is so important to be like clay in God's hands—bendable and moldable.

I didn't know then that Oral and I would go into all the world and preach the Gospel. I didn't know that we would raise up Oral Roberts University with its thousands of young students who could take God's message to the world. In that sense, I really did become a missionary after all!

I'm so glad I decided early to follow God's plan for me, even though it was different from my own. And as you follow God's plan for your life, you'll find that it can be so much better than any plan you envisioned for yourself. His plan is

good, and He can lead you into the greatest joy and fulfill-
ment you've ever known.[60]

make **your** day count

Are you struggling to be someone you're not?
Make a list of your gifts and abilities.
Then make the decision today to be the person God
created you to be and to fulfill His plan for your life.

time **saving** tips

Computer Cleaning

Computers can become very dusty because of static. You can cut static by wiping the exterior of your monitor (not the screen itself unless it is glass) and the surrounding wires and pieces with a cloth dampened with vinegar. Vinegar will de-static these pieces, thus preventing dust from clinging.

Using a half-and-half mixture of either ammonia and water or vinegar and water, you can dampen a cloth to clean the dirtiest portions of your keyboard. This will remove the grease that has been accumulating from your skin. For a more thorough cleaning, use alcohol on a Q-Tip to clean the most detailed pieces of your computer keyboard. (Be especially careful not to allow liquid to seep down into the keyboard.)

If you work with a laptop, the finger touch control pad may become unresponsive or sticky. When the laptop is turned off, dampen a kitchen towel with a little vinegar and wipe all around the control pad. It will become responsive and smooth again.[61]

easy **recipes**

Cornbread[62]

Evelyn Roberts

1 egg
1 cup buttermilk (if regular milk, add 1 tsp. vinegar)
1/4 tsp. baking soda
3 Tbsp. vegetable oil
2 heaping tsp. baking powder
1/2 tsp. salt
1 Tbsp. sugar
1/2 cup flour
1/2 cup cornmeal (yellow—add more meal to make
  batter thicker)

Beat egg in bowl.

Add buttermilk, soda, vegetable oil, salt, baking powder, and
  sugar.

Slowly add flour and then cornmeal. If needed to make batter a
  bit thicker, use more cornmeal.

Heat skillet (an iron skillet is best) and drops of oil. Brush oil
  on bottom and sides of skillet.

Pour batter in skillet, then bake in oven at 400° until brown.

Endure Till You Win

Dr. Patricia D. Bailey

You...must endure hardship as
a good soldier of Jesus Christ.
—2 Timothy 2:3 NKJV

As soldiers of Jesus, we must prepare for battle. Soldiers never go to the front lines without having ever practiced their artillery skills. They prepare ahead of time in boot camp. In fact, the U.S. Special Forces train in more harsh conditions than they will face in the actual war so that in the eye of adversity they won't yield to pressure! We need to be trained to endure hardship in order to win our battles too.

The beauty of God's way is that He always leads us to victory. He will never leave us or abandon us in battle; He is our very present help in times of trouble. He never promised us a trouble-free life, but He did promise to deliver us. When we encounter sorrow and disappointments, we must not carry them; we must go through them and move on. Like Paul exhorted Timothy, we must endure hard times as good soldiers for Jesus

There are some paths that we travel from which the Lord doesn't instantly deliver us, but we cannot cave in! We must endure confidently, knowing that the matter is not *if* God will deliver, but *when* God will deliver. We must possess endurance because it will determine whether we win or lose the battle. And we will win, if we don't give up![63]

make **your** day count

Receive God's grace today to endure whatever battle you are fighting. The Greater One lives in you, and He always causes you to triumph!

The Manifest Presence of God

Lynne Hammond

Blessed (happy, fortunate, to be envied) are those
who dwell in Your house and Your presence;
they will be singing Your praises all the day long.

—Psalm 84:4 AMP

God longs to spend time in intimate communion with you. He wants to make Himself real to you. In fact, the very heart of the Gospel message is the truth that almighty God Himself waits, yearns, and eagerly desires for His redeemed children to come into His presence and fellowship with Him.

The presence of the Lord has always been the central fact of Christianity. I'm not just talking about His presence that dwells inside you because you're born again. I'm talking about the *manifest* presence of God!

God never meant Christianity to be merely a set of rules and regulations, an abstract theory, or an impersonal doctrine. He doesn't want us to have a religion. He wants us to have a relationship with Him! He wants us to know Him personally. He wants us to experience His love so deeply that He becomes dearer to us than anything else in life.

You don't have to settle for a "hearsay Christianity," where you hear someone else talk about his or her experience with God and think that could never happen to you. You can have a firsthand experience of your very own!

That is true Christianity. That's what each of us as believers should have in our relationship with God. Don't settle for anything less.[64]

make **your** day count

Pour out your heart to God today, and let Him
know how much you hunger for His presence.

If My People Will Pray

Lindsay Roberts

If my people, who are called by my name, will humble
themselves and pray and seek my face and turn from
their wicked ways, then will I hear from heaven
and will forgive their sin and will heal their land.
—2 Chronicles 7:14

I believe that we can start a worldwide revival...today! And one way we can do it and bring peace in the midst of chaos is to humble ourselves and pray. Notice that God wasn't talking about the devil's crowd! He said, "If *my* people...."

In the rest of the sentence, He says, "and turn from their wicked ways." We've got sin in our lives, and if we want God to heal us, we need to fall on our faces before God and repent. Instead of spending your days watching some ungodly program or video, consider spending time on your knees before the face of an awesome and powerful God.

The time has come when we've got to be in a place of prayer and a place of prayer covering. These are dangerous times, and we *have* to have a Power Source greater than this world. That Source is Jesus Christ of Nazareth, the Prince of Peace, King of kings, and Lord of lords.

I believe God is calling us together as a body of believers to get the garbage out of our lives. Because when we do, the Holy Spirit of God can rise up inside of us, and we can be a beacon of light to a dark and troubled world. We sing about being a light in darkness. Now let's do it![65]

make **your** day count

Even if it is only five or ten minutes, take some time today to humble yourself and pray for our nation.

time **saving** tips

Tips To Make Your Day Count

Dee Simmons

I remember my mother always saying to me when I was growing up, "You have to get your beauty sleep." And she was right! When I've had eights hours of sleep, I really do look better.

I believe good nutrition and drinking enough water are also important in helping to have younger-looking skin. Here is a simple formula that I use to determine the amount of water I need to drink: I divide my weight in half and drink that amount of water in ounces each day. For instance, 150 pounds divided by 2 equals 75 ounces of water a day.[66]

Mama's Chicken and Mushroom Casserole[67]

4 boneless, skinless chicken breasts
1 can cream of mushroom soup plus 1 can water
Instant Rice
1 cup water

Spray baking dish or pan with no-stick cooking spray.

Place chicken breasts in the pan and cover with 1 can mushroom soup and 1 can of water.

Cover with foil and bake 30 minutes at 300°.

While chicken is baking, boil 1 cup of water and add Minute Rice, following directions on box.

Serve the chicken and mushroom sauce over the rice.

Take Charge of Your Health

Dee Simmons

A cheerful heart is good medicine,
but a crushed spirit dries up the bones.
—Proverbs 17:22

When I was diagnosed with breast cancer in 1987, I let my husband and loved ones take care of me while I was in denial. But as I recovered from a mastectomy and reconstructive surgery, I had a thought that changed everything for me: *It's time for you to take charge. Only you can facilitate your healing process. Others can't do it for you.* I will share the steps I took.

First, slowly and carefully I began to look at those things that may have increased my risk for cancer, such as diet. I decided to reverse bad habits and find real ways to improve my health.

Second, I knew I couldn't afford to be bogged down with negatives, so instead of blaming myself or anyone else, I began to focus on moving ahead toward healing and wellness.

Third, I had to respect myself enough to give myself the best care I could. You can do this by creating healthy habits, such as getting exercise and eating five servings of fruits and vegetables a day.

Fourth, I began to make happiness happen by allowing myself simple pleasures, such as an occasional gourmet coffee treat.

I had to take charge and make each of these things happen, but I did and I have triumphed. You can do them too and experience victory for yourself![68]

make **your** day count

Think of one change you can make today that
will be a step toward total wellness for you.

Does God Hear You?

Suzette Caldwell

This is the confidence that we have in Him, that if we ask
anything according to His will, He hears us. And if we
know that He hears us, whatever we ask, we know that
we have the petitions that we have asked of Him.

—1 John 5:14,15 NKJV

There is a way you can *know* that God hears you when you pray: by praying according to His will. God's Word is His will, so you could say that if we pray according to God's Word, He is listening.

We do this by searching the Scriptures for what God has to say about our situation, then we pray His Word back to Him. For example, I like to pray Psalm 112:1–3 back to God concerning my children: "Father, I praise You. I am blessed because I reverence You. I delight greatly in Your commandments. And because of this, my descendants (here I name my children) are mighty on the earth. They are my generation. I am the upright, and they will be blessed, in Jesus' name. Wealth and riches will always be in their house, and their righteousness will endure forever."

I believe that the Word I have spoken will surround my children as they grow up, and as adults, they will begin to bear fruit from that Word.

Get into God's Word to find out what He has already said about your situation, and then pray that Word back to Him. I believe you can become confident that He hears and answers your prayers![69]

make **your** day count

Find a Bible promise that pertains to a situation you are concerned about, and pray that promise back to God. He will hear you!

What Are You Filling Up On?

Lindsay Roberts

*Above all else, guard your heart, for it is
the wellspring of life.*

—Proverbs 4:23

It is vitally important what we put into our spirits. Because of the society we live in, we can watch movies that are filled with lust, curse words, and pornography. No matter how nicely they try to put it, little to no clothing on people slides into the category of pornography. And when we take all of that into our spirits, we become open to those sinful influences.

Over time we become desensitized to evil. We open our spirits to all the turmoil of the world, because as Christians we don't stop it. And not only do we not stop it, but we *embrace* it by the fact that we watch it and even pay to be entertained by it.

Did you know that the word *video* comes from the Latin word meaning "to envy" or "be jealous"? What are you watching? What videos and video games are you allowing your children to watch? What are you watching on the Internet?

You know, many Christians are well educated, well dressed, well behaved. They declare Christianity with their mouths, but live lifestyles that speak otherwise. First, we have to repent of the garbage and degradation we've allowed into our lives. Then we must vigilantly guard our hearts, so the wellspring of life can flow through us.[70]

make **your** day count

Be especially mindful today of the things you allow your eyes to see and your ears to hear. Fill them with the good things of God's Word.

time **saving** tips

Tips To Make Your Day Count

Becky Wright

Depending on how it is prepared, many of your favorite foods can be good for you. During the holidays, for example, turkey is a wonderful source of protein, sweet potatoes are full of beta-carotene, cranberries are loaded with vitamin C, and even pumpkin pie can have valuable nutrients.

By replacing fat and/or sugar filled ingredients with more healthful alternatives, you may find you like a dish just as well, and you'll be eating healthier in the process.[71]

Lindsay's Favorite Chicken Wings[72]

Lindsay Roberts

2 lbs. chicken wings

$^1\!/_2$ cup brown sugar

$^1\!/_2$ cup granulated sugar

$^1\!/_2$ cup soy sauce

1 cup chicken broth

Wash chicken, pat dry, and set aside.

In baking dish, mix all other ingredients and add chicken. Be sure all pieces are well coated and cover.

Refrigerate to marinate for at least 2 hours.*

Bake uncovered at 400° for 45 minutes. Serve warm or cold.

*I prefer overnight—it's not the same if you marinate less time.

Your First Love

Taffi L. Dollar

I have this [one charge to make] against you: that
you have left (abandoned) the love that you had
at first [you have deserted Me, your first love].

—Revelation 2:4 AMP

Do you remember how you felt when you first became born again and were so in love with Jesus that you had to tell *everyone?* Most likely, however, as time went on, the cares of this world began to wear you down and your joy began to diminish. Rather than asking God for help, you tried to do everything in your own strength. Eventually, you felt too overwhelmed to read the Bible, go to church, or pray.

That's how separation from God begins. All the devil needs is the slightest crack in your foundation to get a foothold, which unchecked becomes a *stronghold;* and your spiritual life, health, finances, and relationships begin to suffer. This is the beginning of the end that Satan has planned for you. (John 10:10.)

My husband, Creflo, says that whatever you give your attention to is what you will desire. Begin to read the Word every day, whether you feel like it or not; it strengthens your spirit. Go to church to get fed the Word at least twice a week. Rise earlier to spend time talking and listening to God.

Though at first you may not *feel* like doing these things, your desire for the things of God will return and your love for Him will grow. Your heart will once again overflow with love for the Lord![73]

make **your** day count

Decide on one thing you can put into practice today to rekindle or strengthen your intimate relationship with God.

Companionship Creates Intimacy in Marriage

Brenda Timberlake-White

The Lord God said, "It is not good
for the man to be alone."
—Genesis 2:18

The Word of God says that when you are married you are no longer two, but you become one flesh. (Eph. 5:31.) That doesn't mean that as individuals you don't have your individual ideas, but when it comes to anything pertaining to you as a couple, you are supposed to blend, speak the same things, do the same things. These things produce intimacy.

If you never do anything together after you get married, then you can forget intimacy. Remember how before you were married the two of you went to the movies and dinner and just enjoyed spending time together? When was the last time you went on a real date? If it's been awhile, perhaps some time away may be in order. How about an overnight stay at a hotel nearby? Enjoy the thrill of rediscovering one another without distraction.

When both of you are at home, let the laundry and chores wait. Stop! Take time to be together. Sit beside one another and enjoy each other's companionship. It's amazing what healing can take place from a touch between friends. It could be a gentle touch on the hand across the table, or perhaps eye-to-eye contact.

Take time to nurture companionship with your mate. Who knows, you may fall in love all over again. Don't put it off. Start today![74]

make **your** day count

Make a date with your spouse. It can be something
as simple as going out for an ice cream cone.
Spending a few minutes alone will be the highlight of your day.

The Power of Taking Authority

Pat Harrison

*Jesus said, "Whatever you bind on earth will be
bound in heaven, and whatever you loose
on earth will be loosed in heaven."*

—Matthew 16:19

I've shed tears and had emotional feelings during my time of transition since my husband, Buddy, went to heaven. You don't live with someone forty years and not have feelings. But I have not experienced loneliness except for one day.

I was sitting in my library reading, when all of a sudden I was aware of this "feeling." I said, "Lord, what is this?" And He said, *The spirit of loneliness is trying to come on you.*

Immediately I said, "I take authority over the spirit of loneliness in the name of Jesus. I will not have it in me or anywhere around me. I do not receive it." Then I began to walk through the house, praying in the Spirit until I had a peace and knew I was free. That spirit of loneliness has never tried to come back.

When a spirit tries to attach itself to you, you must identify it and take authority over it. When something starts happening to you and you try to figure out what it is with your mind, it attaches itself to you more and more. And it stays *until you take authority over it.*

You can take the authority of the Word and set boundaries around you and your family. Declare the Word over your situation. It can set you free from every spirit that is not from God![75]

make **your** day count

Have you sensed something trying to attach itself to you?

Take authority over every evil spirit, forbidding any to have a place in your life.

Baking Substitutions[76]

Nothing is more aggravating than to begin cooking a recipe only to find out you do not have one of the ingredients. Try some of these substitutions:

INGREDIENT	QUANTITY	SUBSTITUTE
Baking powder	1 tsp. double-acting	¼ tsp baking soda + ½ tsp. cream of tartar
Butter	1 cup	1 cup margarine or ⅞ cup lard or shortening + ½ tsp. salt
Buttermilk	1 cup	1 Tbsp. vinegar + sweet milk to make 1 cup or ⅔ cup plain yogurt + ⅓ cup sweet milk
Chocolate	1 ounce	3 Tbsp. cocoa + 1 Tbsp. shortening
Cornstarch (for thickening)	1 Tbsp.	2 Tbsp. flour
Cream	1 cup	½ cup butter + ¾ cup milk
Flour	1 cup all-purpose	1 cup + 2 Tbsp. cake flour
Flour	1 cup cake flour	⅞ cup all-purpose flour
Flour	1 cup self-rising flour	1 cup flour (omit baking powder & salt)
Garlic	1 small clove	¾ tsp. garlic powder
Herbs	1 Tbsp. fresh	1 tsp. dried

Southern Pecan Pie[77]

Pat Harrison

1 cup sugar
3 eggs
2 Tbsp. flour
¾ cup dark corn syrup
2 Tbsp. butter
1 tsp. vanilla
1½ cups of large pecan pieces
Unbaked pie shell

Mix all together and pour into unbaked pie shell.
Bake at 275° to 300° for 1 hour.

There Is Freedom in Christ

Nancy Alcorn

*The Spirit of the Sovereign LORD is on me… He has sent
me to bind up the brokenhearted, to proclaim freedom for
the captives and release from darkness for the prisoners.*

—Isaiah 61:1

Eating disorders, suicide, addictions, unplanned pregnancies. There is an epidemic of social problems that women face today. However, these are more than just problems. They are symptoms of a deeper crisis. Tragically, many women have been deeply wounded by incest, rape, physical and sexual child abuse, and other traumatic experiences.

In order for women to be free, the root causes and not just the symptoms must be dealt with. The main thing to realize is that without a changed heart, there is no such thing as a changed life. Jesus Christ is the only One who can heal a broken heart and bring true freedom.

Women who are dealing with these intense issues need to know that they can be forgiven and receive new life in Christ. And God doesn't just forgive. He is able to provide a way for the shame, guilt, and fear to be removed. A woman's past does not have to destroy her future.

There is no quick fix, however. It is going *through* the painful issues and not around them that produces lasting change. This is where the assistance of a professional Christian counselor can help.

There is hope. Healing is available. Women can come out on the other side fully restored. Freedom can be an experienced reality.[78]

make **your** day count

Are you facing an issue you need to work through?
Don't put it off any longer. Take a step in God's direction today.
Locate a professional Christian counselor, if necessary,
and let the healing begin.

My Greatest Harvest

Lindsay Roberts

They that sow in tears shall reap in joy.
—Psalm 126:5 KJV

Is there an area of your life that seems barren? I know what that feels like. I was told that I'd never have a child. After Richard and I were married, I had two miscarriages and a tumor the size of a grapefruit on my only functioning ovary. After God miraculously removed that tumor and I became pregnant, I endured the death of our firstborn child, Richard Oral, just thirty-six hours after his birth. It was ten long years of heartbreak and failure.

In the midst of my hopelessness, God began to minister to my heart to give baby showers. Learning to plant in famine was one of the hardest things I have ever done in my entire life. But *if you don't plant seed, you will not have a harvest.* One time I had a miscarriage just three days before I gave a baby shower!

I'd serve the cake, give presents, and be so nice. Then after everyone went home, I'd go upstairs and cry until I thought my insides would fall out. But I knew that if I didn't plant in famine, I would always live in famine.

It was hard, but planting those baby showers was worth it. Today, Richard and I have three beautiful daughters, and I can tell you from experience that those who sow in tears *shall* reap in joy![79]

make **your** day count

Is there an area in your life that is barren?

Plant a seed today of the very thing you are believing God to provide.

Time in His Presence

Lynne Hammond

You have made known to me the path of life;
you will fill me with joy in your presence,
with eternal pleasures at your right hand.

—Psalm 16:11

God has tailor-made experiences for you that are peculiar to your specific circumstances. They may not include a Damascus-road experience like the apostle Paul had, but they are exactly what you need to get full of God's presence so you can fulfill His will for your life.

The Lord told me something many years ago that has stood the test of time. He said, *I can change anything about you. I can change your mind. I can change your personality. I can change your emotions. I can change your circumstances. I can change the way you feel about certain things. All you have to do is give Me one thing.*

I got excited when I heard that! I thought, *Surely I can give God one thing!* So I asked, "What is that one thing, Lord?"

Time in My presence, He replied.

Time is the one thing that none of us seems to have. But it is the one thing that God requires of us if we are to walk closely with Him.

You know, God is reasonable. For whatever He has called you to do, that divine call is in itself God's pledge to provide everything you need to stand in that place and to meet every single one of your responsibilities. If God requires something of you, just the requirement itself is His assurance that the means will be provided.

The foundation of your faith will always be in *knowing* God. And you will never know Him well unless you spend much time in His presence, allowing Him to transform you to do His will.[80]

make **your** day count

Set aside some time today for just you and God. Enjoy His presence and fellowship as you would with your very best friend.

More Baking Substitutions[81]

The next time you are cooking and realize you are out of an essential ingredient, try these substitutions:

INGREDIENT	QUANTITY	SUBSTITUTE
Honey	1 cup	1¼ cups sugar + ¼ cup liquid
Milk, whole	1 cup	½ cup evaporated milk + ½ cup water
Milk, sour	1 cup	1 Tbsp. lemon juice or vinegar + sweet milk to make 1 cup
Minced onion (rehydrated)	1 Tbsp. instant	1 small fresh onion
Molasses	1 cup	1 cup honey
Mustard, prepared	1 Tbsp.	1 tsp. dry mustard
Ricotta cheese	1 cup	1 cup cottage cheese + 1 Tbsp. skim milk
Sour cream	1 cup	1 cup yogurt
Sugar, brown	1 cup	¾ cup granulated sugar + ¼ cup molasses
Sugar, powdered	1⅓ cups	1 cup granulated sugar
Yogurt	1 cup	1 cup buttermilk

easy **recipes**

Low-fat Skillet Chicken Pot Pie[82]

1 (10 ¾ oz.) can ⅓-less salt, 99% fat-free cream of
  chicken soup

1 ¼ cups skim milk, divided

1 10 oz. pkg. frozen mixed vegetables

2 cups cooked chicken, diced

½ tsp. ground black pepper

1 cup buttermilk biscuit baking mix

¼ tsp. summer savory (an aromatic mint) or parsley

Heat soup, 1 cup milk, vegetables, chicken, and pepper in
  medium-sized skillet over medium heat until mixture
  comes to a boil.

Combine biscuit mix and summer savory in small bowl.

Stir in 3 to 4 Tbsp. milk, just until soft batter is formed.

Drop batter by tablespoons onto chicken mixture to make
  6 dumplings.

Partially cover and simmer for 12 minutes or until dumplings
  are cooked through, spooning liquid from pot pie over
  dumplings once or twice during cooking.

Garnish with additional summer savory, if desired.

Ready to serve in 25 minutes.

A Double Miracle

Shelley Fenimore

*She said to herself, "If only I may touch His garment,
I shall be made well."*

—Matthew 9:21 NKJV

One evening my husband and I discovered that our nine-month-old daughter, Whitney, was burning up with a 106-degree temperature. Within moments she went into a fibril seizure and then went limp for several minutes. Blood tests revealed that her blood count was 3.5 when it should have been 14—a very serious situation. A blood transfusion was scheduled one week later, but this concerned us greatly because of reports we had heard about blood contamination.

On Friday, we received a prayer cloth from Oral Roberts Ministries. Like the woman with the issue of blood who reached out to Jesus for healing, we used that prayer cloth as our point of contact to reach out for Whitney's healing. She slept with that prayer cloth all weekend, and on Monday, her blood level was back up to 14! She had been healed! Some trying weeks followed, but God brought us through.

Thirteen years later, in 2002, Whitney accompanied a missions team to Mexico, where they encountered a woman who had been blind for three months. Whitney and the others laid hands on the woman, and she instantly received her sight!

Only God knew that Whitney needed her miracle so that years later she could help deliver a miracle to someone else. God sees your future too, so reach out and take the miracle you need today.[83]

make **your** day count

Whatever you need today, find a scripture to use as your point of contact and reach out in faith. Your miracle is on its way!

Single and Successful

Kate McVeigh

You are complete in Him, who is the head
of all principality and power.

—Colossians 2:10 NKJV

God wants you to be successful! Your success in life is not based on your marital status. Just because you are single does not mean you cannot be successful.

Being single also does not mean that you are incomplete. Some people think the definition of the word *single* means "alone," but that's not really what it means. Webster's defines the word *single* as: "...consisting of a separate unique whole...unbroken, undivided...having no equal or like...a separate individual or thing...."[84]

Notice it says, "a separate unique whole." That means you don't have to be married to be a whole person. If you are a Christian, you are complete in Jesus Christ. You are already whole and complete in Him. As far as God is concerned, you can be single *and* successful! You do this by following His plan for your life and obeying Him.

It is important that we do not compare ourselves to others—we each have to follow God's plan for our own individual lives. We each have our own unique path to follow—

we're not called to do the same things. How boring that would be!

If you are single, take heart. God wants you to be successful right now. If you've been holding back waiting around on Mr. Right, start living your life *today* and enjoy the success God has for you.[85]

make **your** day count

No matter how small it is, be successful in something today.

It takes a lot of bricks to build a house.

Your success today is a building block toward a successful future.

Knowing God

Gloria Copeland

Jesus said, "Look! I have been standing at the door and I am constantly knocking. If anyone hears me calling him and opens the door, I will come in and fellowship with him and he with me."

—Revelation 3:20 TLB

It's time to move into a closeness with God where you live separated unto Him and obey Him in all the areas of your life. When we abide in the Lord and His words abide in us, we have living fellowship with God. And it produces great reward.

Knowing God requires a lifestyle of talking to Him and communing with Him. It's listening to Him and obeying what you hear and what you find in His Word. Learning to live in the place where God can talk to you at any moment is the secret to living an overcoming life.

Knowing God should be our number-one priority, because it is the key that opens every supernatural door. Daily intimacy with Him is the way love works. It strengthens you and undergirds your faith. It produces the anointing that enables you to lay hold of all the wonderful things God has provided through Jesus Christ.

Filling your heart with the Word and the voice of God enables you to abide in Him every single day. And as you feast your heart on His promises and His presence, your future will be one of joy and prosperity, healing and health. Instead of chasing after the blessings of God, you'll find they're chasing you and overtaking you at every turn! Understanding this message has changed my life forever.[86]

make **your** day count

Determine to develop intimacy with God today. Let His Word abide in you. Talk to Him throughout the day and listen to what He has to say to you.

time **saving** tips

Healthy Substitutions[87]

Try some of these substitutions to replace fattening, less healthy ingredients in some of your favorite recipes:

INGREDIENT	SUBSTITUTE
Butter	Canola oil, mild olive oil, prune puree, or applesauce
1 ounce chocolate	3 Tbsp. cocoa
Cream or whole milk in batters, muffins, or biscuit doughs	Skim, low-fat, or 1% milk
Cream cheese	Low-fat ricotta + yogurt
Cream cheese in cheesecake	½ whole-milk ricotta + either part-skim ricotta or low-fat (1%) cottage cheese
Sour cream	Plain yogurt
Whipped cream, ice cream to top cakes, pies, warm fruit desserts	Frozen yogurt or low-fat yogurt
1 cup heavy or whipping cream	1 cup evaporated skim milk

easy **recipes**

Susan's Strawberry Jell-O[88]

Gloria Copeland

2 small pkgs. Strawberry Banana Jell-O (or 1 big)
1 ½ cups boiling water
3 or 4 bananas, mashed
1 12-oz. can crushed pineapple, reserving ½ cup juice
1 10-oz. pkg. frozen strawberries
1 cup pecans (optional)

Combine ingredients and refrigerate until firm, then add topping.

Topping:
8 oz. sour cream
8 oz. Cool Whip

Mix sour cream and Cool Whip together and spread over top
of Jell-O.

You Can Hear God's Voice

Evelyn Roberts

[Jesus said], "My sheep recognize my voice;
I know them, and they follow me."
—John 10:27 NLT

Years ago I argued with the Lord because He spoke to Oral audibly but He didn't talk to me that way. But God said to me in my spirit, *I won't talk to you like I talk to Oral because I haven't given you the job that I've given him. I will speak to you in the everyday things of life.* And that is the way the Lord usually speaks to me.

Once in one of Oral's meetings when he directed the people to pray, I said, "Lord, maybe this time You will speak to me audibly." The Lord again spoke to my spirit, but it was as clear as if it had been audible. He said, *You are resisting the Holy Spirit.* Then He said, *If you will go on the long trips with your husband, I will give you your health.*

I had stopped going on long overseas trips with Oral because my feet and legs would swell until I couldn't even feel my feet. However, when Oral planned a trip to the Orient, I chose to obey God and go. When we arrived in Tokyo, I had no swelling whatsoever!

God speaks to most of us in the "everydayness" of life, in a multitude of ways. Whatever way He chooses to communicate with you, it will be a way that is right for you.[89]

make **your** day count

Today, listen for God's voice in the "everydayness" of your life.

He may use a song, a Bible verse, or a note from a friend.

Whatever way He chooses, be sure to thank Him.

The Great Exchange

Lindsay Roberts

God took the sinless Christ and poured into him our sins.
Then, in exchange, he poured God's goodness into us!

—2 Corinthians 5:21 TLB

Jesus left His life in heaven to come to earth so that we could exchange all the hurts, sadness, sickness, and failures in our lives for everything He was and everything He is.

Philippians 4:19 KJV says, "My God shall supply all your need according to his riches in glory by Christ Jesus." Notice, it says "all" your need. Notice that it also says "according to his riches in glory."

God put all the gold and silver in the earth, then He told us to take dominion over the earth and subdue it. Next, He told us that He gives us "power to get wealth" (Deut. 8:18 KJV). But how many of us are using that power?

A while back I agreed to help Richard with a project at Oral Roberts University that ended up costing far more than I had anticipated. But when I went to the Lord, saying, "What have I done?" He answered me with the phrase, *It's only money.* He told me that if I would obey the vision, He would supply the rest. So now when God talks to me about a program, I talk to Him about a *program,* not about money.

Would you like to exchange the life you're living and the mess you're in for all that Jesus is and all that He has for you? Jesus left the streets of gold so you could have it all. He came to give you everything He is in exchange for everything you are![90]

make **your** day count

Are you dealing with a situation that you would like to exchange for God's goodness, love, and provision? Put that thing at the foot of the Cross today and exchange it for the blessing of God.

You Can Master Any Disaster

Cathy Duplantis

In times of disaster they will not wither.

—Psalm 37:19

Jesus mastered every disastrous situation He encountered. He spoke peace to raging seas and they became calm. When an angry crowd tried to hurl Him over a cliff, Jesus just passed through the people and went to the next town. No plan of the devil, no harm, could stop His purpose.

The apostle Paul found himself in a disastrous situation as well. In Acts 27:10 AMP, he warned the crew of the ship he was on that their voyage would be attended with "disaster and much heavy loss." It wasn't long before a horrendous storm ensued. Paul then addressed the crew again, telling them that an angel had spoken to him, assuring him that there would be no loss of life.

Paul went on to say, "I have faith (complete confidence) in God that it will be exactly as it was told me" (v. 25). Even though the storm wasn't over, Paul's faith-filled words restored hope and gave the men courage. Of course, God's words came to pass, and His Word will come to pass in your life too.

Jesus deprived the world of power to harm us. Because of that, we can have cheerful, courageous faith like He did—

even in the midst of disaster. If that is where you find your-self today, be of good cheer. It will not harm you and you will win![91]

make **your** day count

Are you in the midst of a disaster?
Find God's Word regarding your situation, and hold on to it with
cheerful courage, knowing that in the end, the storm will not harm you.

Protection by Listening to Your Spirit

Kellie Copeland Kutz

Your ears will hear a word behind you, saying,
This is the way; walk in it.
—Isaiah 30:21 AMP

When it comes to protecting your children and those you love, it is so important to learn to listen to your spirit. God is always speaking to us. I don't believe one calamity ever happens to us that the Holy Spirit doesn't speak to our spirits beforehand to warn us. John 16:13 says that the Spirit of truth will show us things to come. He knows what the enemy is trying to do. If we are in tune with His voice, He can protect us from the devil's attacks.

I strongly encourage you to pray what I prayed: "Lord, I want to be able to hear You when You speak to me. I want to know what You sound like." God took me to school after I prayed that prayer! He put me through one little exercise after another, and His training caused me to grow light-years in my spiritual walk!

First Peter 5:8 tells us to be sober and vigilant because the enemy walks about as a roaring lion, seeking whom he may devour. Be ever watchful. Keep your spiritual antenna up, always listening on the inside for the Holy Spirit's leading. As you listen to your spirit and heed the Holy Spirit's voice, you can make sure the enemy never has the opportunity to devour you or your family![92]

make **your** day count

Ask God to teach you to recognize and heed His voice today.
Write down what He says to you.

time **saving** tips

Alternative Sweetners

To promote good health, try some of the alternative sweeteners to replace sugar such as honey, molasses, Sucranat, and the herb stevia. All of these are available at health-food stores.

Sucranat is natural, unrefined cane sugar, rich in minerals and vitamins. It can be substituted cup for cup to replace white or brown sugar. It works especially well in baked goods such as oatmeal cookies, carrot cake, banana nut bread, and bran muffins.[93]

Stevia comes in both liquid and powdered form. It is an excellent substitute for sugar and artificial sweeteners because it is a natural herb. Although it is 200-300 times sweeter than sugar, it contains no calories or carbohydrates and it does not appear to trigger a rise in blood sugar. Stevia works especially well in drinks such as coffee and both hot and iced teas.[94]

*It is always a good idea to check with your doctor before incorporating new herbs or supplements into your diet. This is particularly important for diabetics and others sensitive to blood-sugar levels.

Taco Pie[95]

1 pkg. crescent roll biscuit mix (or 1 pkg. crescent rolls)
1 lb. lean ground beef, cooked and drained
    (can also use cooked chicken breasts, cubed)
1 pkg. taco seasoning mix
16 oz. can refried beans
8 oz. fat-free sour cream
Cheddar and mozzarella cheeses, grated
Parmesan cheese

Unroll crescent roll dough into a pie dish.

    Spread dough over bottom and up sides of dish.
    (Makes a flaky crust when done.)

Spread refried beans over the dough.

Sprinkle cooked ground beef mixed with taco mix over the beans.

Spread about half of the sour cream over meat mixture, and
    sprinkle the cheddar and mozzarella cheeses over all.
    (Can also sprinkle a little Parmesan cheese on top.)

Bake at 350° until crust is brown and cheese is melted.
    (The Parmesan cheese will brown the top quickly.)

Top as you would a taco with tomatoes, onions, peppers, salsa,
    and the remaining sour cream.

The Roller-Coaster Ride of Emotions

Joyce Meyer

Jesus Christ…is [always] the same,
yesterday, today, [yes] and forever.

—Hebrews 13:8 AMP

Having emotions is not a sin—it's what we do with them that can get us into trouble. Life is no fun when it is controlled by our feelings because they change—sometimes even moment to moment. Satan tries to use this emotional roller coaster to steal our joy and destroy our effectiveness. In my own life, it wasn't until I got fed up living like a yo-yo and determined that I was not going to live by my feelings, that I finally began to enjoy life.

First, we should aim for emotional stability. Jesus was subjected to the same emotions that we are, yet He did not allow Himself to be moved or led by them. Because He knew He was in God's hands, He had an unshakable sense of peace and security.

Second, we must determine to avoid extreme emotional highs and lows. Staying on a level plain between the two will help us maintain emotional balance. Jesus said in John 15:11 AMP that He wanted His joy and delight—"joy" meaning "calm delight"[96]—to be in us.

The bottom line is that God wants us to keep moving toward Him, lining up our wills with His, and letting Him develop the fruit of self-control within us. He will do a work in you and your circumstances, but you must be determined to control your emotions![97]

make **your** day count

Determine today not to be controlled by your emotions.
Submit your will to God and rely on His grace
to keep you stable, filled with calm delight.

Are You Lonesome Tonight?

Kate McVeigh

May your unfailing love be my comfort,
according to your promise to your servant.
—Psalm 119:76

Maybe you remember Elvis Presley's song "Are You Lonesome Tonight?" But did you know that you can be alone without being lonely? I travel all the time and stay in hotels by myself, but I enjoy being alone and spending time with God, and you can too. He is always there for you, and when you draw near to Him, He will draw near to you. (James 4:8 NKJV.)

You are never really alone. The Holy Spirit lives right inside you and is with you wherever you go! In Matthew 28:20 NKJV Jesus says, "I am with you always, even to the end of the age." In Hebrews 13:5 He says, "Never will I leave you; never will I forsake you." Wherever you go, He is with you.

Maybe you are divorced or widowed or have never been married and you are just lonely. Jesus promised in John 14:18 that He wouldn't leave you comfortless, and in verse 16, He says that He has asked God to give you another Comforter. You can lean on Him when you need comfort.

Going out with a friend of like precious faith can help too. If you don't have a friend like that, ask God to give you one and He will.

Being alone doesn't have to mean you are lonesome. God cares. Go to Him for help.[98]

make **your** day count

Spend a few moments in God's presence and let Him envelop you with comfort. Then go out with a friend and have fun.

Believe the Report of the Lord

Lindsay Roberts

Abraham never wavered in believing God's
promise.... He was absolutely convinced that
God was able to do anything he promised.

—Romans 4:20,21 NLT

What do you do when you get a bad report from the doctor or some other source? If a bad report says one thing but the Word of God says another, *you* decide which report you're going to believe. You can either ignore God's Word, or you can command that bad report to line up with the report of the Lord.

In Genesis 15:5, God told Abraham that he would become the father of many nations. He would have a son and his descendants would be more numerous than the stars in the sky! Abraham was one hundred years old when God said this! Abraham's exceeding age was the *fact*, but fathering a child was *God's report*! And we know the outcome: God's promise came to pass.

If you have received a bad report, get into God's Word regarding your need, then choose to attach your faith to that truth. If you find your faith wavering, be like the man who approached Jesus in Mark 9:24 NLT, saying, "I do believe, but help me not to doubt!" God will help you with any areas of unbelief.

Draw a line in the sand and establish your rights according to the Word of God, and don't waver. Choose to believe the report of the Lord![99]

make **your**
day count

If you have received a bad report,
find a Bible promise regarding that situation.
Draw a line in the sand today and
choose to believe the report of the Lord.

time **saving** tips

Tips To Make Your Day Count

To remove fat from homemade soup, try one of
the following:

Simply add three or four ice cubes and the fat will
congeal around them so you can remove it with a
spoon. You may need to reheat a little when you
are done.[100]

Or, you can refrigerate cooked and cooled soup.
When fat has risen to the top and congealed, break
apart and remove with a spoon. Reheat soup
before eating.

Tortilla Soup[101]

2 boneless chicken breasts

1 small onion, chopped

1 can diced tomatoes and green chilies

$\frac{1}{2}$ tsp. minced garlic

2 Tbsp. oil

2 cans chicken broth

1 can beef broth

1 tsp. cumin

1 tsp. chili powder

1 tsp. salt

$\frac{1}{4}$ tsp. pepper

2 tsp. Worcestershire sauce

1 cup Monterey Jack cheese, shredded

2 cups tortilla strips

Boil chicken until thoroughly cooked and let cool.

Cut chicken into small pieces. Combine chicken, onion, tomatoes, garlic, oil, chicken and beef broths, and all spices.

Simmer for one hour.

In each bowl, place $\frac{1}{2}$ cup tortilla strips, add the soup mixture, and top with cheese.

Serves 4.

Knowing the God of the Word

Lynne Hammond

I gave up all that inferior stuff so
I could know Christ personally.

—Philippians 3:10 THE MESSAGE

Think about it—how many people do you know who can quote scriptures one right after the other, but they don't know Jesus? They may have the *letter* of the Word, but they don't live by the *Spirit* of the Word.

People can easily get off into spiritual error when they live only according to the letter of the Word. A successful walk of faith requires the Word and the Spirit together. Believers need to receive both the impartation of the Holy Spirit and the Word of God preached from the pulpit or spoken personally to their hearts.

Jesus said to the Pharisees, "You search the Scriptures because you think that in them you have eternal life; it is these that testify about Me and you are unwilling to come to Me so that you may have life" (John 5:39-40 NASB).

That's the way religion is. Religious people may seem very devout, but they don't project Christlikeness, love, or compassion to those in need. For instance, when the man with the withered hand came to Jesus in the synagogue on the Sabbath day, those religious people were more interested in keeping their Sabbath day than they were in seeing the man get healed! (Matt. 12:10.) They may have known the Old Testament Scriptures, but they didn't know the *Spirit* of the Scriptures.

It's important to know the Word of God, but we need to know the God of the Word too. That's real Christianity.[102]

make **your** day count

Is your relationship with God alive and real, or has it become dead and religious? Ask God for a fresh impartation of His Spirit today.

Healed of Cancer

Dodie Osteen

He sent forth his word and healed them;
he rescued them from the grave.

—Psalm 107:20

On December 10, 1981, I was diagnosed with metastatic cancer of the liver. I was told I only had a few weeks to live, even if I pursued treatment.

As the head of our house, my husband, John Osteen, anointed me with oil. Together we took authority over any disease and cancerous cells in my body. That was on December 11, 1981, the day I believe my healing began.

In spite of every discouraging symptom and the enormous fear that would come against me, my heart knew that God's Word promised healing and His Word could not lie. If I had not had confidence in that, I would have died. But day by day, I clung to my Bible and its healing promises. The Word became my life, and it healed me.

The Word of God is extremely important to people who are fighting a battle with their health, for often it's the only hope they have. I am so thankful to be alive today and to be able to bring you a message of hope! You can win the battle against sickness. I did not get healed because I am special. I was healed because I dared to take God at His Word. You can do that too. And what God did for me, He'll also do for you.[103]

make **your** day count

Are you or is someone you know facing sickness today?
Claim one of the many healing scriptures found in the Bible.
Dare to take God at His Word today. You are healed!

The Word Always Produces Fruit

Marilyn Hickey

I send [my word] out and it always produces fruit.
It shall accomplish all I want it to, and prosper
everywhere I send it.

—Isaiah 55:11 TLB

I was a rebellious Christian at the time my husband and I first met. I was especially rebellious against the baptism of the Holy Spirit and God's perfect will for my life. I just wasn't interested—there seemed to be so many more exciting things to do in life.

I loved to be with Wally and wanted to do exciting things with him. The only place he ever went, however, was to church or out for dinner. He wouldn't take me dancing. He really didn't even take me to movies! I wanted to see him, so I had to go to church—even if I didn't want to!

Church was dull. But Wally was exciting. Little did I realize that God would use the Word from those supposedly dull services to give me a hunger for the baptism of the Holy Spirit! Wally was also praying and fasting for me, so my rebellious nature was soon broken. I was then baptized in the Holy Spirit.

Each day I grew more and more in the wisdom of our Lord. How I delight today in His Word. When you begin to hear God's Word, it works its way into your heart![104]

make **your** day count

Pray as King David did: "Open my eyes that I may see wonderful things in your law" (Ps. 119:18), and spend some time in God's Word today.

Fearfully and Wonderfully Made

Pat Harrison

I praise you because I am fearfully and wonderfully made;
your works are wonderful, I know that full well.

—Psalm 139:14

You are a woman by birth—God does not make mistakes. Rejoice that He skillfully crafted you, and understand that it is okay to be the unique individual He has created you to be.

I know about this from personal experience. I had a difficult time learning that it was all right to be me. When I was younger, I was shy, introverted, and easily intimidated. I set no boundaries with others, so people felt free to walk all over me.

I could not function the way I needed to as long as fear and torment ruled my life. I had to find out that it was okay to be who I was and to set boundaries. I had to learn what I liked and didn't like and that I wanted things to be according to God's Word. I had to allow the Word of God and the Holy Spirit to change me.

Instead of trying to please people, focus on pleasing God first. Allow Him to work in you and change you into that person He intended. He has specifically called *you* to be and to do certain things, but He will never ask you to be someone you cannot be.

Discover the real you. Then be the best you that you can be.[105]

make **your** day count

Decide today not to allow the opinions of others to determine who you are. Be who God made you to be.

time **saving** tips

Eating Out Tips

Marty Copeland

- Drink a protein drink, such as the one on the next page, or eat half a sandwich with a bottle of water one-half to one full hour before dinner.

- If going straight from work, for example, pack a healthy snack to help curb your appetite before you get there.

- Drink water before your meal comes.

- Order a salad instead of eating chips and dip.

- Order baked, broiled, or grilled entrées instead of fried.

- Drink unsweetened tea or coffee.

- Call ahead and ask what healthy choices are available.

- Split your meal with a friend or your spouse.

- Instead of butter, try I Can't Believe It's Not Butter®, or top potatoes with cottage cheese or salsa. Try veggies sautéed in olive oil.

- Order fruit for dessert.[106]

easy **recipes**

My Favorite Protein Drink[107]

Marty Copeland

8 oz. organic skim milk
6–8 ice cubes
$\frac{1}{2}$ or 1 whole banana
1 scoop Nature's Plus Spiru-tein Powder
  (I like the chocolate flavor)

Barlean's Flaxseed Oil:
1 Tbsp. for a weight-loss program
2 Tbsp. for weight maintenance
2 squirts of ConcenTrace Mineral Drops

Double Your Treasure

Lindsay Roberts

Even today I [the Lord] declare that
I will restore double to you.

—Zechariah 9:12 NKJV

Richard and I received a prophecy in 2003 that God was going to give our ministry a double portion of His blessing. We were led to the verse above as well as Deuteronomy 28:12 AMP which says, "The Lord shall open to you His good treasury, the heavens...to bless all the work of your hands." We immediately began rejoicing, but we also realized that there were things we would have to do to get ready to receive God's doubling of our treasure.

First of all, it's important to rid our lives of anything that might be polluted by the devil. Then we confess it and ask God to forgive us and cleanse us, so we can receive the new refreshing He wants us to have.

Matthew 6:21 NKJV says that "where your treasure is, there your heart will be also." If God wants to double your treasure, what is it that's going to get doubled? Whatever is hidden in your heart—good or bad—because according to God's Word, *that* is your treasure.

Psalm 35:27 says that God takes pleasure in the prosperity of His children. I believe God wants to double our treasure through His Word, His will, and His abundant supply in every area of our lives. But let's get our hearts ready and be in the right position to receive His double-portion blessing![108]

make **your** day count

Examine your heart to determine what treasure is in your heart. If you need to make adjustments, do it today and get ready to receive the double-portion blessing God wants to give you.

Protecting Your Children Through Discipline

Kellie Copeland Kutz

Children, obey your parents in the Lord, for this is right.
"Honor your father and mother...that it may go well
with you and that you may enjoy long life on the earth."

—Ephesians 6:1–3

There's no way around it. The Word says that if your children are going to live long on the earth, they have to obey their parents. That doesn't just happen automatically. You have to teach them to be obedient, and the only way to do that is to discipline them.

God laid out the perfect system in His Word for disciplining your children. Interestingly, He doesn't even mention "time-outs." Actually, the only form of parental discipline the Word really talks about is spanking—and that's the one kind of discipline the world says not to use!

What amazes me is that so many believers have agreed with the world on this subject. They say, "Well, the Bible is outdated in its instructions on discipline." Not surprisingly, these Christians are also reaping the same results in their children that the world is—disobedience, disrespect, and rebellion.

I haven't found any truth in the Bible that has passed away, and that includes God's instructions on parental discipline.

You can't believe God for something apart from His Word. You have to obey what His Word says; only then are you in a position to believe God for the desired results—children who grow up to be obedient, respectful, a lot of fun—and continually protected from all harm![109]

make **your** day count

If you are a parent, go over Ephesians 6:1–3 with your children.
Teach them that there is great reward when they
honor and obey you—long life on the earth.

Step by Step to Victory

Julie Wilson

In his heart a man plans his course,
but the LORD determines his steps.
—Proverbs 16:9

Lindsay Roberts and I are longtime friends. Many years ago we both delivered babies at the same time at the City of Faith hospital. Afterward, Lindsay went in for her well-baby checkup and everything was fine. My well-baby checkup was with the same doctor, but my baby was not fine. In fact, we were told that he had cancer and a liver that was seven times larger than normal.

Times like this are why we must have a personal relationship with the Lord. I didn't have a clue that the diagnosis was coming, but it was no surprise to God. I praise God for the doctors who helped my child, but they didn't know the perfect plan. Only God knew that. Doctors often know what works, but only God knew for sure what would work for my son. The doctors gave their diagnosis, but we appealed to the higher court of God's final judgment.

We asked God to show us the perfect path through the trial and to help us walk in it. That is the only thing that produces victory. We chose to utilize the best that medicine had to offer, while at the same time, we continued to pray.

So many people prayed and stood with us, and God healed my son.

Ask God to reveal His perfect path to your victory. Step by step, follow it, and you will win.[110]

make **your** day count

Ask the Lord to show you the next step in your miracle journey.
Take that one step today!

Hope Is Powerful Medicine

Dee Simmons

May the God of hope fill you with all joy and peace
as you trust in him, so that you may overflow
with hope by the power of the Holy Spirit.

—Romans 15:13

I call *hope* the world's most powerful medicine. Though science can't measure its effects and no one can absolutely assess its power, most doctors can recall at least one "incurable" patient who, for unknown and unsuspected reasons, slid over into the winner's column. Often clinicians attribute such results to something intangible they call *hope*. Virtually everyone I have talked to, doctor and patient alike, has spoken about the important role hope plays in achieving healing.

The staff of the famous Menninger Foundation identified hope to be of primary importance in treating the emotionally disturbed. They could immediately discern when a patient turned that crucial corner, because hope changes all of us for the better.

Hope helps us heal, and it literally powers our future. It is also contagious. Hope in a patient raises hope in others, and it tends to spread quickly from one person to another. We should all intentionally spread this potent medicine to those around us.

Hope enables us to envision our healing and to expect and focus on success. Faith strengthens the inner person as we learn to trust God and expect Him to provide for specific personal needs.

With God, there is always reason to hope. So look up. Something good is right around the corner for you.[111]

make **your** day count

No matter how dark things may appear, there is always hope.
Focus on the God of hope today, and
let Him lead you to your brighter tomorrow.

My Story

Nancy Alcorn

There is a way that seems right to a man,
but in the end it leads to death.

—Proverbs 14:12

Shortly after becoming a Christian and graduating from college, I innocently fell into the struggle of my life.

One evening a couple had me over for dinner. Afterward I volunteered to clean their house while they attended a meeting. I began to feel nauseated from overeating, but I also had a strong desire to please my friends. No matter how nauseated I was, I kept trying to clean. Finally, I decided that my only hope of fulfilling my commitment was to make myself throw up, thus eliminating the nausea.

After I had "helped myself," it hit me that I could do that all the time, eat anything I wanted, and still control my weight. I began purging several times a week, which led to many physical problems. Even worse were the all-consuming thoughts about food and the overwhelming fear of gaining weight.

It was a five-year period of hell so bad that at times I wished I had been dead. But somehow, I knew there was hope in God. There was, but it was only through dealing with the root causes. Because I stayed in the Word, renewed my mind to the truth, and cried out to God continuously, I

was eventually set free. Thankfully there is more help for
eating disorders today. It isn't easy, but Christ can set the
captive free. [112]

make **your** day count

Is there any area in your life where you are being held captive?
Begin today to declare that the freedom Christ purchased is yours—now!
And if you need extra support, talk to a pastor or godly counselor.

time **saving** tips

Tips To Make Your Day Count

To help a cake rise higher, make sure that all the ingredients are at room temperature before you begin.

When making a cake or something comparable from a mix, instead of coating the pan with flour, use a bit of the dry mix along with butter or margarine. It will prevent sticking equally well and will not look white after the cake/item is baked.[113]

Cream Cheese Pound Cake

Betsy Williams

1 cup magarine

½ cup butter (or 1 ½ cup butter total)

8 oz. cream cheese

2 ½ cups sugar

Dash salt

2 tsp. vanilla

6 large eggs

3 cups sifted flour

Soften first three ingredients and beat well.

Add remaining items, mix, and pour into greased/floured Bundt pan.

Start in cold oven. Bake at 275° for 90 minutes to 2 hours, until golden and inserted knife comes out clean.

Let God Multiply Your Mustard-Seed Faith

Evelyn Roberts

*[Jesus said], "I tell you the truth, if you have faith as
small as a mustard seed, you can say to this mountain,
'Move from here to there' and it will move.
Nothing will be impossible for you."*

—Matthew 17:20

This verse shows us that you can't just go out to the mountain—which represents your need—and say, "Move!" You've got to do something first: Plant a seed of your faith. *Then* you can say to your mountain, "Move!"

A mustard seed is about the size of a grain of salt, but if you plant it, it grows into a tree so big that birds can nest in its branches. (Matt. 13:32.) In the same way, the seed of faith you plant can be small, but when God takes it and multiplies it, it becomes something great enough to uproot mountains of problems and move them out of your way!

We saw this truth in action when, early in her marriage, Lindsay's doctor told her, "You have a tumor on your ovary that's like a mountain."

Lindsay exclaimed, "Oh, praise You, Jesus!" because she knew that Jesus had said she could speak to her mountain and command it to *move* out of her way!

To make a long story short, Lindsay had planted seeds of faith, and she told her mountain to move! When the doctor operated, there was no tumor to be found! *The mountain was gone!*

God's Word assures us that we can have faith that will move the mountains in our lives as we plant seeds of faith.[114]

make **your** day count

What mustard seed of faith could you plant today? After you do it, command whatever mountain is standing in your way to move! in Jesus' name.

Plunging Into the Deep!

Lindsay Roberts

He must increase, but I must decrease.

—John 3:30 KJV

In Ezekiel 47, Ezekiel had a vision in which he was led to a river of life where the water got deeper and deeper until finally, he couldn't cross it unless he swam.

If you think of the anointing of God as a river of life, many of us live in ankle-deep water. The problem is, the remaining 99 percent of your body is exposed as a target for Satan! It's easy to live in ankle-deep water at first. You can still maintain control and be dignified because you're not wet all over. Then God begins to call you deeper.

Knee-deep water is a little harder because of the water resistance, but you can still get back to shore. Here you're getting a little more of the Word. Then God calls you into shoulder-deep water. That's okay, though, because your head is still above water. You're still in control.

But that's the problem. *You* are still in control! God is saying, "Take the plunge!" When you totally submerge yourself into God's ways and His Word, then you're no longer exposed; all your flesh is covered. You become immersed in God's ideas and God's ways.

So take the plunge into the things of God! Cover yourself with the anointing. You'll wonder why you waited so long.[115]

make **your** day count

Think of an area of your life where you have maintained control.
Take the plunge today by giving up that control
and making Jesus Lord of that area.

"He Told Me You Were Coming!"

Dr. Patricia D. Bailey

The eyes of the LORD range throughout the earth to
strengthen those whose hearts are fully committed to him.
—2 Chronicles 16:9

It's easy to be faithful when God "calls" you to *the masses;* however, He desires the same level of faithfulness when He assigns you to *the one.*

Years ago I had gone to Zimbabwe to minister to church leaders, but deep inside I knew that there was a particular woman to whom God was sending me. After finishing my official obligations, I traveled into the rural regions, instructing the driver to just drive—that I would know when we reached her.

Finally, I was drawn to a particular village. Word spread quickly that Americans had come, and a woman began shouting, "I knew you were coming—He told me you were coming!"

Nearly eighty, "Mama Mutare" then told me, "I have given my life to the Lord…. With God's help, I have nearly converted every surrounding village." She then asked me to pray that God would use her and send her help to reach the unreached remote villages in the area.

I possessed something that Mama Mutare desired, and she was not going to allow me to leave without her portion.

Through this, I learned that God can speak to His children wherever they are and give them the ability to hear His instructions. More importantly, Mama Mutare taught me that *ministry is serving people* and being willing to be obedient to serve *the one!*[116]

make **your** day count

Be on the lookout for the one to whom God would have you minister today.

It's Time to Reclaim God's Blessing!

Lindsay Roberts

All who put their faith in Christ share the same
blessing Abraham received because of his faith.

—Galatians 3:9 NLT

It's sad, but I have found that Christians are among the sickest, poorest people in the world, and that's the complete opposite of what God wants for us. We have a Bible right to claim God's blessing!

Throughout the Bible, God gave His people His blessing, but they kept messing it up. Finally, God sent His Son to die so that the blessing of Abraham might come upon all those who believe in Christ Jesus. (See Gal. 3:13,14.)

Instead of embracing God's blessing, however, we've let Satan slowly but surely infiltrate our world. There's a constant spiritual battle raging for our minds, our families, and our finances as Satan works to separate us from God.

Today the world has its own music, money, power, television, and voice; and we Christians have let all of this permeate our lives. We are allowing the world to train up our children. Is it any wonder that we have lost some of our blessing?

Now I believe it's time for us as the Body of Christ, to stand up and say, "Stop it! That's enough, in Jesus' name!"

The blessing that God first gave to Abraham is ours, but we have to do our part. Give God our tithes, accept His Son's saving grace, take our stand against Satan, and then reclaim God's blessing.[117]

make **your** day count

Reclaim your blessing by personalizing Galatians 3:13,14.
"Christ redeemed me from the curse of the law by becoming
a curse for me.... He redeemed me in order that the blessing
given to Abraham might come to me through Christ Jesus."

time **saving** tips

Tips To Make Your Day Count

Although not recommended, sterling and silver plates may be washed in an automatic dishwasher; however, the pieces should be removed before the intense heat of the drying cycle starts.

If you choose to put these items in the dishwasher, note that sterling and silver-plate flatware should never be washed together with stainless flatware.[118]

Suzanne's Chicken Spaghetti [119]

Gloria Copeland

2 fryers
1 12-oz. box thin spaghetti
1 onion, chopped
1 green pepper, chopped
Butter to sauté
3 cans soup (cream of mushroom, cream of chicken, or
   cream of celery)
1 can mushrooms
1 can chopped pimientos
½ lb. Old English cheese
½ lb. Velveeta

Boil fryers.
Remove fryers and soak spaghetti in broth. Drain, saving broth.
Bone fryers.
Sauté onion and pepper.
Mix all ingredients together.
Place in a greased casserole dish. Bake 45 minutes at 375°.
Serves 16. Freezes well.
May use 2 casseroles. Extra broth can be used for thinning.

The Fruit of the Spirit

Sharon Daugherty

The fruit of the Spirit is love, joy, peace, longsuffering,
kindness, goodness, faithfulness, gentleness, self-control.
—Galatians 5:22,23 NKJV

When you receive Jesus into your heart, His life and nature come to live in you. Your old way of life ceases to exist, and a new life begins. "If anyone is in Christ, he is a new creation; old things have passed away; behold, all things have become new" (2 Cor. 5:17 NKJV).

Galatians 2:20 NKJV says, "I have been crucified with Christ; it is no longer I who live, but Christ lives in me." Now that He's in you, He is working on you to will and do what pleases God. (Phil 2:13.) You're not trying to live your life by your own strength. He's now in you to help you live your life. John 1:16 NKJV says, "And of his fullness we have all received, and grace for grace." When Jesus came into your heart, you received *all* of His nature and *all* of His fruit. They abide in you *now!* However, like a baby is born into the world as a baby and has to grow to become an adult, you're born into God's kingdom as a baby and you grow into spiritual maturity. Growth is a process. Don't get down on yourself because you're learning to walk.

A parent doesn't condemn a toddler for falling when that child is making the effort to walk. Instead, that parent will encourage the child to get up and walk again. God doesn't condemn you when you mess up, but He will encourage you to get up and walk again. The more you walk, the easier it will become. Walking requires you to renew your thinking according to His Word and then submit to His Holy Spirit's prompting within you, showing you what to do or say and what not to do or say. *Walking* in the fruit of the Spirit is a choice. You might think that it is unattainable, but by renewing your mind to God's Word, you can walk in His fruit and nature. (Rom. 12:1,2; Col. 3:10; Eph. 4:23,24.)

In John 15:4 NKJV, Jesus says, "Abide in Me, and I in you. As the branch cannot bear fruit of itself, unless it abides in the vine, neither can you, unless you abide in Me."

An amazing thing is that over a period of years, the branches that grow on a grapevine begin to look like the vine itself. Likewise, as you and I (the branches) continue in the Word of God (the Vine), we will begin to look like Jesus and bear abundant fruit.[120]

make **your** day count

Ask the Holy Spirit to guide you to a verse for this day.
"Abide" in that verse and allow it to "abide" in you today.
You will bear fruit.

Faith Is a Magnet

Lynne Hammond

We ought always to thank God for you, brothers, and
rightly so, because your faith is growing more and more.
—2 Thessalonians 1:3

Once when I was praying about faith, God reminded me of an experiment I had done in my eighth-grade science class. In this experiment, I had a tissue filled with little metal particles that looked like grains of sand. I took all of those particles and spread them out on two big sheets of notebook paper.

Next I put a little magnet on that paper, and it pulled a few of those little particles around it. Then I did the same thing with progressively larger magnets, and they attracted increasing numbers of particles. The last magnet was like a big brick. It started pulling all of those particles to itself before it had even gotten close to the paper!

After God reminded me of this experiment, He said, *Faith is very much like a magnet. The larger and stronger that magnet is, the more it will pull in.*

Faith pulls things from the unseen realm into the seen realm. The stronger your faith, the further you can reach into the spirit realm to pull God's gifts into the physical and mental realms. As you nourish your spirit with the pure milk and strong meat of the Word, like the larger and larger magnets, your spirit will be able to "pull in" everything God has provided for you.[121]

make **your** day count

Spend some time feasting on God's Word today.
It will help you develop and strengthen your faith.

Things That Helped Me Win the Battle Over Cancer

Dodie Osteen

In all thy ways acknowledge him,
and he shall direct thy paths.

—Proverbs 3:6 KJV

On December 10, 1981, I received a death sentence—metastatic cancer of the liver. My weight had dropped to eighty-nine pounds, and I was extremely weak and exhausted. But God's Word healed me. I want to share the things that helped me. I believe they will help you too.

- Many prayed for me, but I realized that faith for my healing was a personal matter between Jesus and me.

- I dressed normally every day, never going to bed to be cared for by others.

- My husband and I prayed the prayer of agreement.

- I chose life and pleaded my case before God.

- I examined my heart and made things right with people whom I had offended.

- I did things that inspired a positive, hopeful attitude, like putting out pictures of myself when I had been the picture of health.

- I prayed for others.

- I clung to my Bible and the healing scriptures to fight my doubts and the thoughts from the devil.

- I maintained a positive confession, even when I was very afraid and wavering in my mind.

- My family stood with me and treated me as though I were well.

Over time I became stronger and stronger until finally, I was totally healed of cancer. I am still free today, and you can be too.[122]

make **your** day count

Are you fighting a hard battle?
Ask God to reveal the steps that lead to your victory.

Abide in the Peace of God

Pat Harrison

[Jesus said], My [own] peace I now give and bequeath to
you…. [Stop allowing yourselves to be agitated and
disturbed; and do not permit yourselves to be fearful
and intimidated and cowardly and unsettled.]

—John 14:27 AMP

To walk in God's supernatural peace, you have to keep
your mind tranquil and worry-free. It is easy for you to keep
your *spirit* in peace because Jesus, the Prince of Peace, abides
there. Your mind, on the other hand, is often another matter.

Jesus understands mental anguish because He identified
completely with humanity and shared every aspect of human
existence. (Heb. 2:14,15.) He was beaten, ridiculed, misun-
derstood, despised, rejected, and betrayed. His family
thought He was crazy. His disciples deserted Him in His hour
of need.

On the cross, Jesus suffered every mental attack you could
ever face. He bore all that and suffered for you because He
loves you so much. He made it possible for you to have a
tranquil heart and mind in every circumstance.

It takes effort to walk in supernatural peace. Reading the
Word aloud and hearing yourself speak it is effective because
it leaves no room for unrest or disturbing thoughts. You must

continually put the Word into your mind to keep it in agreement and at peace with your spirit.

Circumstances cannot take God's peace from you unless you let them. You do not have to become agitated, cowardly, intimidated, disturbed, and unsettled. Take hold of that peace that passes understanding. It belongs to you.[123]

make **your** day count

Refuse to accept worrisome, fearful, or disturbing thoughts today.
Instead, rest in God's peace, knowing
He is working things out for your good.

Love and Healing

Dee Simmons

These three remain: faith, hope and love.
But the greatest of these is love.

—1 Corinthians 13:13

Without any doubt, love helps us heal. Doctors observe the potent effects of the connection between love and medicine. I believe love is as necessary to healing as any amount of clinical expertise, state-of-the-art treatments, or the newest drugs or surgical techniques. When we are sick and scared, we need love and lots of it.

So what can you do to express your love to someone who is fighting a life-threatening illness? Remember:

- Your love is needed and essential.

- You are a part of the patient's healing process.

- Follow your heart.

- Be willing to schedule time to do the small tasks that mean so much, and do them with great love.

- Gentleness and quiet companionship are like a soothing balm.

- Love boldly. Do not fear rejection.

- Write one- or two-sentence love notes to hide in books, drawers, or bathrobe pockets for your loved one to discover.

- Read aloud. Choose beautiful, short, inspiring passages.

- Smile often. Gently touch your loved one's skin, hold his hand, smooth her hair. Stay connected.

Walking through a serious illness with someone is not easy, but that is when the person needs you the most. Your love can make a difference.[124]

make **your** day count

Whether you know someone with a serious health concern
or you see someone who is just having a rough day,
take the opportunity to express your love today.

Passing the Stress Test

Lindsay Roberts

*Count it all joy when you fall into various trials, knowing
that the testing of your faith produces patience. But let
patience have its perfect work, that you may be perfect and
complete, lacking nothing. If any of you lacks wisdom,
let him ask of God...and it will be given to him.*

—James 1:2–5 NKJV

Are you under enormous pressure? God has not called
you to be stressed, frustrated, or upset. Let's look at what the
Word of God says about what you can do to take control of
stress and pass the stress test.

First, count it all joy. You do it because you know this:
that the trying of your faith works patience, and when
patience has had its perfect work, you will be left wanting
nothing! I believe that when we count it all joy, it causes God
to come on the scene and Satan to go the other direction.

Second, remember that God is working in you. Let
patience have her perfect work. Most people think patience is
waiting and doing nothing until something happens. Not
true! Patience means hopeful endurance, tolerance, diligence,
self-possessed waiting, and dogged tenacity.

Third, ask for wisdom. Notice that we do the asking and
God does the answering.

There are many great scriptures to help you deal with stress, but until you apply them, they might as well be fairy dust to you. It's time to decide, "I will not react to stress and fall apart, but I will respond with the Word of God!" Choosing the right attitude in the middle of stress can bring the answers from the Lord.[125]

make **your** day count

In whatever stressful situation you find yourself today, declare, "I will not let stress overtake me. I count it all joy, and I will patiently endure so that I will lack nothing!"

About the Author

Lindsay Roberts and her husband, Richard, were married in 1980. She began traveling with her husband, ministering throughout the world and supporting him in what the Lord has called him to do.

"After the birth of our son, Richard Oral," Lindsay says, "we were devastated when he lived only 36 hours. But God picked us up, dried our tears, and helped us try again." Out of that experience from pain to victory, Lindsay wrote *36 Hours with an Angel*—the story of how God sustained their faith after Richard Oral's death and blessed her and Richard with the miracle births of their three daughters: Jordan, Olivia, and Chloe.

Lindsay hosts *Make Your Day Count*, a daily television program full of ministry, cooking, creative tips, and lots of fun. With her husband, Richard, she also cohosts the nightly television program, *The Hour of Healing*.

She has coauthored several books, such as *A Cry for Miracles* and *Dear God, I Love To Eat, But I Sure Do Hate To Cook* cookbook. She has also written several children's books, including *ABC's of Faith for Children* and *God's Champions*.

Lindsay serves as editor of *Make Your Day Count*, a quarterly magazine aimed at today's woman; *Miracles Now*, a quarterly magazine for ministry partners; and *Your Daily Guide to Miracles*, a daily devotional book published semi-annually.

She is also a member of the Oral Roberts University Board of Regents.

"I am dedicated to God and willing to do whatever He calls me to do," Lindsay says. "I also stand in support of the call of God upon my husband. He and I are both grateful that God is using us for His glory."

Royalties from the sale of this book and others
in the *Make Your Day Count* series will go towards
the Make Your Day Count Scholarship Fund.

To contact Lindsay Roberts
or request a free issue of the
Make Your Day Count magazine,
please write to:

Lindsay Roberts
c/o Oral Roberts Ministries
Tulsa, Oklahoma 74171-0001
or
e-mail her at:
Lindsay@orm.cc

Please visit the *Make Your Day Count* Web site at
www.makeyourdaycount.com.

*Please include your prayer requests
and comments when you write.*

If you would like to have someone join in agreement with you
in prayer as a point of contact, consider calling the Abundant Life
Prayer Group at 918-495-7777. They are there to pray with you
twenty-four hours a day, seven days a week.

About the Contributors

Nancy Alcorn is president and founder of Mercy Ministries of America, a residential facility for troubled girls ages 13-28. Presently, Mercy Ministries operates homes and licensed adoption agencies in various cities around the world. Plans are underway to open additional homes in the United States and in other countries. To contact Nancy, call (615) 831-6987 or visit www.mercyministries.org.

Dr. Patricia D. Bailey is a lecturer, author, and founder of Master's Touch Ministries International, a mission outreach. M.T.M. has also founded Y.U.G.O. (Young Adults United for Global Outreach) and Sister to Sister, an international outreach to women in foreign countries. Dr. Bailey serves as a missions strategy consultant to several growing churches and has developed leadership programs around the world. Master's Touch Ministries has headquarters in Atlanta, Los Angeles, and London, England. Dr. Bailey is the proud mother of a son, Karim Israel Bailey. To contact Patricia, call (770) 521-0373 or visit www.mtmintl.org.

Billye Brim is an author, editor, and anointed preacher of the Gospel and has been a Lindsay Roberts Women's Conference speaker. After the homegoing of her husband in 1986, the Lord led Billye to study Hebrew in Israel, and now she takes Christians to Israel at least twice a year to see modern-day Israel through Jewish eyes. Bible prophecy is an important part of Billye's teaching with an emphasis on the Glory of God and His Glorious Church. To contact Billye, please call (417) 336-4877 or visit www.billyebrim.org.

Deborah Butler is the first lady of Word of Faith International Christian Center in Southfield, MI; Word of Faith Christian Center in San Antonio, TX; and Faith Christian Center in Phoenix, AZ, where she serves in ministry with her husband, Bishop Keith A. Butler. She is a licensed and ordained minister, serving as the director of Women of Virtue fellowships and has been a Lindsay Roberts Women's Conference speaker. She and Bishop Butler have three children: Rev. Keith A Butler II and his wife, Minister Tiffany Butler, Minister MiChelle Butler, and Minister Kristina Butler. To contact Deborah, call (248) 353-3476 or visit www.wordoffaith-icc.org.

Suzette Caldwell and her husband, Kirbyjon Caldwell, pastor a congregation of fifteen thousand at Windsor Village United Methodist Church in Houston, Texas. A graduate from the University of Houston, she is an anointed teacher of God's Word and has committed her life to achieving excellence through biblical living. To contact Suzette, call (713) 551-8617 or visit www.kingdombuilders.com.

Gloria Copeland is an author, teacher, and ordained minister alongside her husband, Kenneth Copeland. Together they've reached millions around the world with the message that God's Word works. Gloria has been a Lindsay Roberts Women's Conference speaker, and in 1986, she received an Honorary Doctorate of Humane Letters from Oral Roberts University. In 1994, she was voted Christian Woman of the Year. You may contact Gloria by calling (800) 600-7395 or visiting www.kcm.org.

Marty Copeland is a certified personal trainer, fitness instructor, and nutritional guidance counselor. She is a wife and mother of three children. For more information on **weight loss** and **fitness products** you may contact Marty at **www.martycopeland.com** or by calling (800) 600-7395.

Sharon Daugherty co-pastors alongside her husband, Pastor Billy Joe Daugherty at Victory Christian Center in Tulsa, Oklahoma. In 1976, Sharon earned a Bachelor's Degree in Music Education from Oral Roberts University. She is an anointed worship leader, psalmist, author, and teacher and has been a Lindsay Roberts Women's Conference speaker. The Daughertys are involved in outreaches through TV, radio, literature, and crusades in the United States and in other nations. She and her husband have four children. To contact Sharon, call (918) 491-7700 or visit www.victorytulsa.org.

Taffi L. Dollar and her husband, Dr. Creflo A. Dollar Jr., pastor World Changers Church in College Park, Georgia, where she serves as the vice president of the ministry, president and CEO of Arrow records, and overseer of the Women's Fellowship. Taffi is an author and teacher and has been a Lindsay Roberts Women's Conference speaker. Taffi earned a bachelor's degree in Mental Health and Human Services from Georgia State University. To contact Taffi, visit www.worldchangers.org or call (770) 210-5850.

Cathy Duplantis is a fiery, anointed minister of the Gospel who is dedicated to living by faith and teaching others to do the same. Among her many ministry opportunities, she has been a Lindsay Roberts Women's Conference speaker. The wife of Evangelist Jesse Duplantis, Cathy has worked with her husband in the ministry, serving as administrator, editor-in-chief of *Voice of the Covenant* magazine, and television co-host. To contact Cathy, call (985) 764-2000 or visit www.jdm.org.

Shelley Fenimore has appeared on *Make Your Day Count* as a guest and as a co-host several times. She and her husband, Rick, a graduate of Oral Roberts University, reside in Tulsa, Oklahoma, with their three children. They are longtime partners with Oral Roberts Ministries.

Lynne Hammond is nationally known for her teaching and writing on prayer. She and her husband, Mac, are founders of Living Word Christian Center in Minneapolis, Minnesota. Under Lynne's leadership at Living Word, the prayer ministry has become a nationally recognized model for developing effective "pray-ers." To contact Lynne, call (763) 315-7200 or visit www.mac-hammond.org.

Pat Harrison is known as a woman who loves the Holy Spirit. She is a successful author, speaker, and leader whose ministry encourages people to develop a personal walk with God and get to know the person of the Holy Spirit. Pat is a member of the Oral Roberts University Board of Regents and has been a Lindsay Roberts Women's Conference speaker. Pat and her late husband, Buddy, founded Faith Christian Fellowship International in Tulsa, Oklahoma. The ministry is affiliated with over three thousand churches worldwide. To contact Pat, call (918) 492-5800 or visit www.fcf.org.

Marilyn Hickey's mission is to "cover the earth with the Word," which has been effectively accomplished through worldwide speaking, writing, television, and the establishment of a fully accredited two-year Bible college. In 1986, Marilyn received an Honorary Doctorate of Divinity from Oral Roberts University. She is Chairman of the Oral Roberts University Board of Regents, a member of the International Charismatic Bible Ministries Board of Trustees, and has been a Lindsay Roberts Women's Conference speaker. Marilyn is married to Wallace Hickey, pastor of Orchard Road Christian Center in Greenwood Village, Colorado. They have two grown children. You may contact Marilyn by calling (303) 770-0400 or visiting www.mhmin.org.

Kellie Copeland Kutz is a speaker, author, musician, wife, and mother of four. She directs the development of all Kenneth Copeland Ministries' children's product and is the contributing editor for *Shout! The Voice of Victory for Kids*, a monthly children's magazine. She is best known as Commander Kellie—the fearless, faith-filled adventurer in the *Commander Kellie and the SuperKids*ₛₘ videos, audio series, and novels. To contact Kellie, visit www.kcm.org or call (800) 600-7395.

Kate McVeigh is known as a solid evangelist and teacher of the Gospel, with a powerful anointing to heal the sick and win the lost. A graduate of Rhema Bible Training Center in Tulsa, Oklahoma, her outreach includes books, teaching tapes, a daily radio broadcast, and a weekly television broadcast. Kate's down-to-earth and often humorous teaching of the Word motivates many to attain God's best for their lives. To contact Kate, call (586) 795-8885 or visit www.katemcveigh.org.

Joyce Meyer has helped multiplied thousands experience the victory that Jesus died for them to have. She has accomplished this through hundreds of meetings across the country, an extensive audio and video library, fifty-four books, and her radio and television broadcasts. In 1998, Joyce received an Honorary Doctorate of Divinity from Oral Roberts University, and she serves as a member of the International Charismatic Bible Ministries Board of Trustees. Joyce has also earned a PhD in Theology from Life Christian University in Tampa, Florida. She and her husband, Dave, the business administrator at Joyce Meyer Ministries, reside in St. Louis, Missouri, and are the parents of four children. To contact Joyce, call (800) 727-9673 or visit www.joycemeyer.org.

Dodie Osteen, wife of the late Pastor John Osteen, has a mighty ministry of love and compassion. Healed of cancer by standing on God's Word, she has inspired hope and faith in countless numbers of people. In 1991, Dodie received an Honorary Doctorate of Humane Letters from Oral Roberts University. She is also a registered nurse. To contact Dodie, visit www.lakewood.cc or call (713) 635-4154.

Terri Copeland Pearsons and her husband, George, are pastors of Eagle Mountain International Church. The eldest daughter of Kenneth Copeland, Terri leads the prayer life at EMIC. She also ministers and travels on behalf of her father for Kenneth Copeland Ministries and her husband, George, for Eagle Mountain International Church throughout the United States and internationally as well. To contact her, call (800) 660-7395 or visit www.emic.org.

Colleen Rickenbacher is a Certified Meeting Professional and a Certified Special Events Professional who has been in the hospitality industry for over thirty years. Fifteen of those years have been with the Dallas Convention & Visitors Bureau, covering all areas including sales, services, member services, and vice president of event planning. She is also a dynamic speaker and trainer who personalizes presentations around your specific goals. To contact Colleen call (214) 571-1040 or visit www.colleenrickenbacher.com.

Evelyn Roberts, wife of Evangelist Oral Roberts, has been by his side in the ministry for over fifty years. Mrs. Roberts is Lindsay Roberts' mother-in-law. She is the author of several books and is a Lifetime Spiritual Regent on the Oral Roberts University Board of Regents. She is also a member of the International Charismatic Bible Ministries Board of Trustees and has been a speaker at the Lindsay Roberts Women's Conferences. Mrs. Roberts attended Northeastern State University in Oklahoma and Texas College of Arts and Industries in Kingville, Texas, and taught school three years before marrying Oral. They are the parents of four children; thirteen grandchildren, one of whom is in heaven; and thirteen great-grandchildren. For more information, visit www.orm.cc.

Patricia Salem has been a partner with Oral Roberts Ministries since the 1950s, when she was miraculously healed of cancer through reading one of Oral Roberts' books. She moved to Tulsa in the eighties, after her daughter, Lindsay, entered the Oral Roberts University School of Law. In 2003, Patricia received an Honorary Doctorate of Divinity from Oral Roberts University, and she can be seen with Lindsay daily on the *Make Your Day Count* television broadcast. For more information, visit www.orm.cc.

Dee Simmons is a member of the Oral Roberts University Board of Regents and has been a Lindsay Roberts Women's Conference speaker. She is founder and chairman of her own nutrition company, Ultimate Living International, a nutritional product manufacturer and distributor. Her daily nutritional program, *Health Views*, is seen across the nation. Dee has been the national spokesperson for Making Memories Breast Cancer Foundation since 1999. To contact Dee, call (214) 220-1240 or visit www.ultimateliving.com.

Brenda Timberlake-White graduated with honors from Fayetteville State University in Fayetteville, North Carolina, in 1971 and Bread From Heaven Bible Institute in 1981. She and her husband, the late Bishop Mack Timberlake, served as the senior pastors of Christian Faith Center in Creedmoor, North Carolina. Following the passing of her husband, Brenda accepted the mantle to serve as senior pastor. She is a member of the International Charismatic Bible Ministries Board of Trustees and has been a Lindsay Roberts Women's Conference speaker. She is a governor on the Board of Governors for the National Center for Faith-based Initiatives and is the proud mother of four daughters and three sons. To contact Brenda, call (919) 528-1581 or visit www.timberlakeministries.com.

Betsy Williams is a freelance editor/writer, specializing in inspirational books. Her work has appeared in publications from a variety of publishers in the Christian bookselling industry, including several major publishers. Originally from Huntsville, Alabama, she is a 1983 graduate of Rhema Bible Training Center in Tulsa, Oklahoma, where she and her family currently reside. Betsy and her husband, Jim, are the proud parents of two active boys. She may be contacted at williams.services.inc@cox.net.

Julie Wilson is a native of Pittsburgh, Pennsylvania. She and her husband, Jim, are both graduates of Oral Roberts University and are Certified Public Accountants in Tulsa, Oklahoma. She is a regional representative with Stonecroft Ministries and often speaks to Christian Women's Clubs throughout the country. She and Jim have three sons.

Becky Wright is a registered, licensed nutritionist with extensive clinical experience using nutrition as supplementary therapy in cancer treatment. She earned a degree in nutrition from Iowa State University. Becky serves as nutrition spokesperson for Cancer Treatment Center in Tulsa, where she teaches weekly nutrition classes. For more information on Cancer Treatment Centers of America, call (800) 615-3055 or visit their national Web site at www.cancercenter.com.

Endnotes

1   Lindsay Roberts, *Make Your Day Count* magazine (Tulsa, OK: Oral Roberts Evangelistic Association, Oct.-Dec. 2002) pp. 6-7.

2   Joyce Meyer, *Miracles Now* magazine (Tulsa, OK: Oral Roberts Evangelistic Association, Nov.-Dec. 2000) pp. 22-23.

3   Terri Copeland Pearsons, "An Ambassador of Love" (Ft. Worth, TX: Kenneth Copeland Ministries) <http://www.kcm.org/studycenter/*articles*/relationships/ambassador_love.html> (accessed Sept. 2003).

4   Dee Simmons, *Make Your Day Count* magazine (Tulsa, OK: Oral Roberts Evangelistic Association, April-June 2001) pp. 13-14.

5   Dee Simmons, tips and recipe from *Make Your Day Count* broadcast (Tulsa, OK: Oral Roberts Evangelistic Association).

6   Taffi L. Dollar, *Changing Your World* magazine, "Loving the Woman in the Mirror" (College Park, GA: Creflo Dollar Ministries, March 2002) pp. 5-6.

7   Evelyn Roberts, *Make Your Day Count* magazine (Tulsa, OK: Oral Roberts Evangelistic Association, April-June 2001) p. 7.

8   "Helpful Tips and Hints," <http://www.baycooking.com/kitchen_tips.htm> (accessed Oct. 2003).

9   Evelyn Roberts, *Richard & Lindsay Roberts Family Cookbook* (Tulsa, OK: Oral Roberts Evangelistic Association, 1990).

10 Marilyn Hickey, *He Will Give You Another Helper* (Tulsa, OK: Harrison House Inc., 2001) pp. 229-230.

11 Lindsay Roberts, *Make Your Day Count* magazine (Jan.-March 2003) pp. 7-8.

12 Kate McVeigh, *The Blessing of Favor* (Tulsa, OK: Harrison House, Inc., 2003) pp. 3-12.

13 Gloria Copeland, *Go with the Flow* (Tulsa, OK: Harrison House, Inc., 2001) pp. 5-9.

14 "Herbs and Spices," <http://www.baycooking.com/kitchen_tips.html>, (accessed Sept. 2003).

15 Gloria Copeland, *Richard & Lindsay Roberts Family Cookbook* (Tulsa, OK: Oral Roberts Evangelistic Association, 1990).

16 Marty Copeland, "More Than a New Year's Resolution" (Ft. Worth, TX: Kenneth Copeland Ministries) <http://www.kcm.org/studycenter/articles/health_healing/more_than_resolution.html> (accessed Sept. 2003).

17 Cathy Duplantis, *How To Behave in a Cave* (Tulsa, OK: Harrison House, Inc., 2000) pp. 5-6, 12.

18 Patricia Salem, *Make Your Day Count* magazine (Oct.-Dec. 2002) p. 9.

19 Colleen Rickenbacher, *Make Your Day Count* broadcast (Sept. 29, 2003).

20 Patricia Salem, *Richard & Lindsay Roberts Family Cookbook.*

21 Mack and Brenda Timberlake-White, *Heaven on Earth in Your Marriage* (Tulsa, OK: Harrison House, Inc. 1993) pp. 7-13.

22 Lindsay Roberts, *Make Your Day Count* magazine (July-Sept. 2002) pp. 6-7.

23 Patricia Salem, *Make Your Day Count* magazine (July-Sept. 2002) p. 26.

24 Transportation Security Administration, "Time Saving Tips," <http://www.tsa.gov/interweb/assetlibrary/Time_Saving_Tips.doc> (accessed Oct. 2003).

25 Patricia Salem, *Richard & Lindsay Roberts Family Cookbook.*

26 Billye Brim, *Make Your Day Count* magazine (July-Sept. 2003) pp. 8-9.

27 Lindsay Roberts, *Make Your Day Count* magazine (April-June 2001) pp. 9-12.

28 *Make Your Day Count* magazine (Aug.-Dec. 2002) pp.20-21

29 Tips on removing ballpoint pen, <http://www.tipking.com/Tips/publish/tip_61.html> (accessed Oct. 2003).

30 Gloria Copeland, *Richard & Lindsay Roberts Family Cookbook.*

31 Dodie Osteen, "Time for a Turn Around" (Houston, TX: Lakewood Church) <http://www.lakewood.cc/resources_find_beginning.html> (accessed Sept. 2003).

32 *Merriam-Webster OnLine Dictionary*, copyright © 2002, s.v. "thrive"; available from <http://www.m-w.com>.

33 Cathy Duplantis, *Voice of the Covenant* magazine, "God Wants You To Thrive, Not Just Survive!" (New Orleans, LA: Jessie Duplantis Ministries, May 2003) pp. 18-20.

34 Sharon Daugherty, *The Spirit-Filled Mother's Guide to Total Victory* (Tulsa, OK: Harrison House, Inc., 1994) pp. 131-136.

35 Sharon Daugherty, *Richard & Lindsay Roberts Family Cookbook.*

36 Deborah Butler, *Make Your Day Count* magazine (May-June 2001) pp. 28-29.

37 Lindsay Roberts, *Miracles Now* (Sept.-Oct. 2000) p. 21.

38 Evelyn Roberts, *Miracles Now* (April-June 2003) p. 6.

39 "Kitchen Tips," <http://www.baycooking.com/kitchen_tips.html> (accessed Oct. 2003).

40 Evelyn Roberts, *Richard & Lindsay Roberts Family Cookbook*.

41 Patricia Salem, *Make Your Day Count* magazine (Jan.-March 2003) p. 14.

42 Billye Brim, *Make Your Day Count* magazine (July-Sept. 2003) p. 10.

43 Kellie Copeland Kutz, "Make Sure Your Children Are Protected," www.kcm.org (accessed Sept. 2003); *Protecting Your Family in Dangerous Times* (Tulsa, OK: Harrison House, Inc. 2002) pp. 11-18.

44 Sharon Daugherty, *Walking in the Fruit of the Spirit* (Tulsa, OK: Sharon Daugherty) pp. vii-ix.

45 The Augustine Club at Columbia University, "Twenty Time-savers" (New York, NY: 2000) <http://www.columbia.edu/cu/augustine/study/time.html> (accessed Oct. 2003).

46 Sharon Daugherty, *Richard & Lindsay Roberts Family Cookbook*.

47 Marty Copeland, "The Body/Finance Connection"; http://www.kcm.org/studycenter/articles/health_healing/more_than_resolution.html (accessed Sept. 2003).

48 Lindsay Roberts, *Make Your Day Count* magazine (Oct.-Dec. 2002) p. 6.

49 Taffi L. Dollar, *Make Your Day Count* magazine (July-Sept. 2003) pp. 12-13.

50 Patricia Salem, *Make Your Day Count* magazine (July-Sept. 2003) p. 15.

51 DoItYourself.com, <http://doityourself.com/clean/homemadestainremovers.html> (accessed Oct. 2003).

52 Patricia Salem, *Richard & Lindsay Roberts Family Cookbook*.

53 Joyce Meyer, *Life in the Word* magazine (Fenton, MO: Life in the Word, Inc./Joyce Meyer Ministries, July 2003) pp. 5-6.

54 Gloria Copeland, *Make Your Day Count* magazine (June 2001) pp. 30-31.

55 Dr. Patricia D. Bailey, "Finishing Touches" Introduction.

56 FC&A Publishing Online, <http://www.fca.com/articles/QC201.html> (accessed Oct. 2003).

57 Terri Copeland Pearsons, "An Ambassador of Love"; <http://www.kcm.org/studycenter/articles/relationships/ambassador_love.html> (accessed Sept. 2003).

58 Lindsay Roberts, *Make Your Day Count* magazine (April-June 2003) pp. 6-8.

59 Marilyn Hickey, *Daily Devotional* (Denver, CO: Marilyn Hickey Ministries, 1985) p. 214.

60 Evelyn Roberts, *Miracles Now* (July-Sept. 2003) p. 9.

61 Tipking.com (accessed Oct. 2003).

62 Evelyn Roberts, *Richard & Lindsay Roberts Family Cookbook*.

63 Dr. Patricia D. Bailey, *Finishing Touches* (Tulsa, OK: Harrison House, Inc. 2003) Chapter 21.

64 Lynne Hammond, *Renewed in His Presence* (Tulsa, OK: Harrison House, Inc. 2001) pp. vii-viii.

65 Lindsay Roberts, *Make Your Day Count* magazine (Tulsa, OK: Oral Roberts Evangelistic Association, Oct.-Dec. 2001) p. 8.

66 Dee Simmons, *Make Your Day Count* magazine (Oct.-Dec. 2002) p. 25.

67 *Make Your Day Count* broadcast.

68 Dee Simmons, *Make Your Day Count* magazine (April-June 2003) pp. 28-29.

69 Suzanne Caldwell, *Make Your Day Count* magazine (April-June 2003) pp. 30-31.

70 Lindsay Roberts, *Make Your Day Count* magazine (Oct.-Dec. 2001) p. 7.

71 Becky Wright, *Make Your Day Count* magazine (Oct.-Dec. 2003) pp. 14-15.

72 Lindsay Roberts, *Richard & Lindsay Roberts Family Cookbook*.

73 Taffi L. Dollar, "Your First Love" (College Park, GA: *Changing Your World Magazine,* Sept. 2002) <http://www.creflodollarministries.org/pdf/sept02.pdf> (accessed Sept. 2003).

74 Mack and Brenda Timberlake-White, *Heaven on Earth in Your Marriage,* pp. 43-45.

75 Pat Harrison, *Miracles Now* (Sept.-Oct. 2000) p. 15.

76 Aunt Edna's Kitchen, "Commonly Used Substitutions"; <http://www.homecooking.about.com/gi/dynamic/offsite.htm?site=http://www.auntedna.com/utils/substitutions.html> (accessed Oct. 2003).

77 Pat Harrison, *Richard & Lindsay Roberts Family Cookbook*.

78 Nancy Alcorn, *Mercy for Eating Disorders* (Tulsa, OK: Harrison House Publishers) pp. 11-15.

79 Lindsay Roberts, *Make Your Day Count* magazine (Oct.-Dec. 2001) p. 34.

80 Lynne Hammond, *Renewed in His Presence,* pp. 39-41.

81 Aunt Edna's Kitchen, "Commonly Used Substitutions"; <http://www.homecooking.about.com/gi/dynamic/offsite.htm?site=http://www.auntedna.com/utils/substitutions.html> (accessed Sept. 2003).

[82] *Dear God, I Love to Eat…but I Sure Hate to Cook!* (Tulsa, OK: Lindsay Roberts, 2001) p. 36.

[83] Shelley Fenimore, *Hour of Healing* broadcast #1423 (Tulsa, OK: Oral Roberts Evangelistic Association) aired March 3, 2003.

[84] *Merriam-Webster OnLine Dictionary,* copyright © 2002, s.v. "single," and "SINGULAR"; available from <http://www.m-w.com>.

[85] Kate McVeigh, *Single and Loving It* (Tulsa, OK: Harrison House Inc., 2003) pp. 3-4.

[86] Gloria Copeland, *To Know Him* (Tulsa, OK: Harrison House, Inc., 2003) pp. 1-2.

[87] About, Inc.,"Lighter: Healthy Substitutions for Baking"; <http://www.homecooking.about.com/gi/dynamic/offsite.htm?site=http://www.foodwine.com/food/egg/egg0196/lightsub.html≥ (accessed Oct. 2003).

[88] Gloria Copeland, *Richard & Lindsay Roberts Family Cookbook*, p. 51.

[89] Evelyn Roberts, *Miracles Now* (March-April 2000) p. 11.

[90] Lindsay Roberts, *Miracles Now* (March-April 2000) p. 14.

[91] Cathy Duplantis, *Voice of the Covenant* (June 2003) pp. 18-20.

[92] Kelli Copeland Kutz, "Make Sure Your Children Are Protected," www.kcm.org (accessed Sept. 2003); *Protecting Your Family in Dangerous Times* (Tulsa, OK: Harrison House, Inc. 2002) pp. 6-8.

[93] Naturalife Health Ltd., Co. Wicklow, Ireland, <http://www.naturalife.ie/hdocs/shop_udo.html≥ (accessed Oct. 2003).

[94] Excerpt from *The Body Ecology Diet* by Donna Gates, <http://www.holisticmed.com/sweet/stv-cook.txt> (accessed Oct. 2003).

[95] *Make Your Day Count* broadcast.

[96] James Strong, "Dictionary of the Words in the Greek Testament" an *Exhaustive Concordance of the Bible* (Nashville: Abingdon, 1890), p. 77, entry #5479, s.v. "joy," John 15:11.

[97] Joyce Meyer, *Life in the Word* magazine (Aug. 2001) pp. 14-15.

[98] Kate McVeigh, *Single and Loving It,* pp. 89—92.

[99] Lindsay Roberts, *Miracles Now* (July-Sept. 2003) pp. 10-11.

[100] "Kitchen Tip", <http://www.baycooking.com/kitchen_tips.html>; (accessed Oct. 2003).

[101] *Make Your Day Count* broadcast.

[102] Lynne Hammond, *Renewed in His Presence,* pp. 52-53.

[103] Dodie Osteen, *Healed of Cancer* (Houston, TX: John Osteen, 1986) pp. 5, 14, 20-21, 24-25, 43.

[104] Marilyn Hickey, *Daily Devotional,* p. 338.

[105] Pat Harrison, *The Great Balancing Act* (Tulsa, OK: Harrison House, Inc. 2002), pp. 3-6.

[106] Marty Copeland, *Higher Fitness—Marty's Top Ten Diet and Fitness Strategies,* "10 Eating Out Tips," excerpt at <http://www.kcm.org/studycenter/articles/health_healing/eatout_tips.html>.

[107] Ibid.

[108] Lindsay Roberts, *Miracles Now* (April-June 2003) pp. 10-11.

[109] Kellie Copeland Kutz, "Make Sure Your Children Are Protected," www.kcm.org (accessed Sept. 2003); *Protecting Your Family in Dangerous Times* (Tulsa, OK: Harrison House, Inc. 2002) pp. 9-10.

[110] Julie Wilson, *Make Your Day Count* #1834 (aired 3/20/03).

[111] Dee Simmons, *Surviving Cancer* (Tulsa, OK: Harrison House, Inc., 2001) pp. 21, 26, 28, 187.

[112] Nancy Alcorn, *Mercy for Eating Disorders,* pp. 43-47.

[113] Baking tips, <http://www.baycooking.com/kitchen_tips.html> (accessed Oct. 2003).

[114] Evelyn Roberts, *Miracles Now* (Sept.-Oct. 2000) p. 7.

[115] Lindsay Roberts, *Miracles Now* (Sept.-Oct. 2000) p. 14.

[116] Dr. Patricia D. Bailey, *Finishing Touches,* Chapter 21.

[117] Lindsay Roberts, Make Your Day Count magazine (Tulsa, OK: Oral Roberts Evangelistic Association, July-Sept. 2003) p. 11.

[118] Pamphlet on care for stainless flatware, Lenox, Inc.

[119] Gloria Copeland, *Richard & Lindsay Roberts Family Cookbook.*

[120] Sharon Daugherty, *Walking in the Fruit of the Spirit,* pp. vii-ix, 165-167.

[121] Lynne Hammond, *When Healing Doesn't Come Easily* (Tulsa, OK: Harrison House, Inc. 2000) p. 47.

[122] Dodie Osteen, *Healed of Cancer,* pp. 18-23, 25-29, 32-34.

[123] Pat Harrison, *The Great Balancing Act,* pp. 69-74.

[124] Dee Simmons, *Surviving Cancer,* pp. 157, 169.

[125] Lindsay Roberts, *Miracles Now* (Nov.-Dec. 2000) pp. 14-15.

Other Books in the
Make Your Day Count Devotional Series

Make Your Day Count Devotional for Mothers
Make Your Day Count Devotional for Teachers
Make Your Day Count Devotional for Teens

Additional copies of this book
are available from your local bookstore.

If this book has been a blessing to you
or if you would like to see more of the
Harrison House product line,
please visit us on our Web site at
www.harrisonhouse.com.

HARRISON HOUSE
Tulsa, Oklahoma 74153

The Harrison House Vision

Proclaiming the truth and the power

Of the Gospel of Jesus Christ

With excellence;

Challenging Christians to

Live victoriously,

Grow spiritually,

Know God intimately.